J O H N
S T O T T

A Summary of his Teaching

To David Reed
with best wishes

led
9-14-21

JOHN STOTT

A Summary of his Teaching

Ted Schroder

P QUANT
editions

First published in 2021 by Piquant Editions, Manchester, UK
www.piquanteditions.com

ISBNs
978-1-909281-88-2 Print
978-1-909281-89-9 Mobi

British Library Cataloguing-in-Publication Data
A catalogue record of this book is available in the UK from the British Library.
ISBN 978-1-909281-88-2

Cover and Book Design by projectluz.com

Contents

Publisher's Note

The particular editions of John Stott's works that the author quotes from, abbreviates, paraphrases or summarizes, are listed in the Endnotes. Several titles are now out of print (OP). The Bibliography lists as far as possible current in-print editions of John Stott's works; most OP works continue to be accessible in Logos Bible Software.

Commentaries that John Stott wrote in the BST and Tyndale series have in this book been referred to by the name of the Bible book(s) they expound.

The Author and Publisher acknowledge with thanks permission by the following publishers to reproduce extracts from their works in this book:

- InterVarsity Press, Downers Grove and Westmont, IL, USA — **www.ivpress.com**
- Inter-Varsity Press, London, England — **https://ivpbooks.com**
- Wm. B. Eerdmans Publishing Company, Grand Rapids, MI, USA — **www.eerdmans.com**
- Langham Literature, Carlisle, UK — **https://langhamliterature.org**
- Hodder & Stoughton, London, England — **www.hodder.co.uk**

Particular permissions for extracted quotes include:

From *Baptism and Fullness* by John Stott. Copyright © 1964 John R.W. Stott. Used by permission of Inter-Varsity Press, London, England.

From *Basic Christianity* by John Stott. Copyright © 1958 John R.W. Stott. Used by permission of Wm. B. Eerdmans, Grand Rapids, MI, USA and Inter-Varsity Press, London, England.

From *Between Two Worlds / I Believe in Preaching* by John Stott. Copyright © 1982 John R.W. Stott. Used by permission of Wm. B. Eerdmans, Grand Rapids, MI, USA. Permissions for *I Believe in Preaching* appear with the individual extracts.

From *Christian Basics*. Permissions appear with the individual extracts.

From *Christ in Conflict* (originally published as *Christ the Controversialist*) by John Stott. Copyright © 1970 J.R.W. Stott. Used by permission of InterVarsity Press, P.O. Box 1400, Westmont, IL 60515 USA and Inter-Varsity Press, London, England. Revised edition copyright © 2013 Executors of the Literary Estate of John R.W. Stott, P.O. Box 296, Carlisle, CA3 9WZ, UK.

From *The Contemporary Christian* by John Stott. Copyright © 1992 John R.W. Stott. Used by permission of Inter-Varsity Press, London, England.

From *The Cross of Christ* by John Stott. Copyright © 1986 John R.W. Stott. Used by permission of InterVarsity Press, P.O. Box 1400, Westmont, IL 60515, USA and Inter-Varsity Press, London, England.

From *Essentials* by David L. Edwards & John R.W. Stott. Permissions appear with the individual extracts.

From *Living Church* by John Stott. Copyright © 2007 John R.W. Stott. Used by permission of Inter-Varsity Press, London, England.

From *The Message of Ephesians* (BST) by John Stott. Copyright © 1979 John R.W. Stott. Used by permission of Inter-Varsity Press, London, England.

From *The Message of Galatians* (BST) by John Stott. Copyright © 1968 John R.W. Stott. Used by permission of Inter-Varsity Press, London, England.

From *The Message of the Sermon on the Mount* (BST) by John Stott. Copyright © 1978 John R.W. Stott. Used by permission of Inter-Varsity Press, London, England.

From *The Preacher's Portrait*. Copyright © 1961 J.R.W. Stott. Copyright © 2016 Executors of the Literary Estate of John R.W. Stott, P.O. Box 296, Carlisle, CA3 9WZ, UK. Used by permission of Langham Publishing, Carlisle, UK.

From *What Christ Thinks of the Church*. Copyright © 1958 J.R.W. Stott. Copyright © 2019 Executors of the Literary Estate of John R.W. Stott, P.O. Box 296, Carlisle, CA3 9WZ, UK. Used by permission of Langham Publishing, Carlisle, UK.

Introduction

While there have been several biographies of John Stott written and selections of his writings compiled, there has not been, to my knowledge, any "systematic theology nor even a full and balanced exposition of his thought and teaching."[1]

I was fortunate to have been called by John Stott to be his curate (assistant minister) at All Souls Church, Langham Place, London, when I graduated from Cranmer Hall, Durham University in 1967. My training in Christian ministry was begun under his guidance. At 26 years old, I came to live with him in the Rectory at 12 Weymouth Street and occupied the bed-sitting room next to his on the third floor. He shared his files with me, supervised my pastoral visiting, and delegated to me the responsibility of ministry to young business and professional people, students, the poor, the elderly, nursing-home residents, and other church members. It was to be the beginning of a lifelong mentoring that informed and inspired me over the years. When I moved to the United States he asked me to establish and chair the American branch of the Langham Foundation, and he continued to visit. Over many years, he preached for me in the congregations where I ministered, in Massachusetts, Florida, and Texas. I cherish my library of his published works, many of whom he sent me inscribed as gifts. His thought and life heavily influenced my theology. So it is with deep thankfulness for what I received from him that I set out to compile my understanding of his teaching in this way, hoping to make it accessible for the benefit of others who labor in congregational ministry. In this I do not claim any academic qualifications for my perspective but only those of a journeyman pastor.

I have endeavored to read everything that John Stott wrote from the beginning of his ministry and everything that he edited and contributed to – approximately sixty publications. I then divided his teaching into a number of areas of Christian theology, as reflected in the chapter titles of this book, and attempted to summarize his contribution. While Stott did not write a systematic theology, his theological approach was consistently biblical, evangelical, and comprehensive over the years of his ministry. He took his cue from Charles Simeon (1759–1836), the renowned Vicar of Holy Trinity Church in Cambridge for 53 years, who rejected systems of Christian theology. So greatly did Stott revere him, he hung a portrait of Simeon in his study. William Carus, the memoirist of Simeon, characterized his approach in the following way.

As for names and parties in religion, he equally disclaims them all: he takes
his religion from the Bible; and endeavors, as much as possible, to speak as
that speaks. Hence, as in the Scriptures themselves, ... there will be found
sentiments, not really opposite, but apparently of an opposite tendency,
according to the subject under discussion. ... He is aware, that they who are
warm advocates for this or that system of religion, will be ready to condemn
him as inconsistent: but if he speaks in exact conformity with the Scriptures,
he shall rest the vindication of his conduct simply on the authority and
example of the Inspired Writers. He has no desire to be wise above what is
written, nor any conceit that he can teach the Apostles to speak with more
propriety and correctness than they have spoken.[2]

Daniel Wilson, Bishop of Calcutta, made similar points about Simeon that
can be equally applied to Stott.

Moderation on contested and doubtful points of theology contributed to
his ultimate success – not moderation in the sense of tameness as to the
great vital truths of the Gospel – not moderation as implying conformity to
the world's judgment of Christian doctrine – but the true Scriptural moderation arising from a sense of man's profound ignorance and the danger
of attempting to proceed one step beyond the fair and obvious import of
Divine Revelation. In this sense he was moderate. A reverential adherence
to the letter of inspired truth was the characteristic of his preaching. He
never attempted to push conclusions from Scripture into metaphysical re-
finement. Unless the conclusions themselves as well as the premises, were
expressly revealed, he was fearful and cautious in the extreme. He conceived
early in life the design of forming a school of Biblicism, if the term may be
employed. Instead of detaching certain passages from the Bible, deducing
propositions from these passages, and then making these propositions the
starting posts of his preaching, he kept the Bible as his personal standard;
and used articles of theology for the end for which they were intended, not
to supersede the Bible, but to be a centre of unity, a safeguard against heresy
and error, and a means of discipline and order in the church. He did not
consider it his duty to attempt to reconcile all the apparent difficulties in
St. Paul, but to preach every part of that great apostle's doctrine in its place
and bearing, and for the ends which each part was evidently employed by
its inspired author. Here shone forth that wisdom in Mr. Simeon's character to which we have already adverted – the wisdom of bowing before the
infinite understanding of the Almighty, and not venturing to speculate on
matters placed far above human comprehension.[3]

This moderation and reluctance to speculate caused Stott to weigh all interpretations of Scripture fairly and to offer his own opinion based upon the

context of the passage. He drew his conclusions after rational consideration of the arguments and not from contrived consistency with systematic theologies. This sometimes resulted in taking positions that were unpopular with other evangelical theologians, who were not reluctant to point out his seeming inconsistencies. He was willing to acknowledge his agnosticism about contested points of doctrine where others insisted on being dogmatic. He preferred to focus on the chief doctrines of the faith, rather than be led into idle speculation about things he felt were peripheral and open to disagreement. He would often quote the phrase he attributed to Richard Baxter:

> In essentials unity;
> in non-essentials liberty;
> in all things charity.

It is not surprising, therefore, that Stott's best-selling book, *Basic Christianity*, has been translated into 50 languages (22 more are in progress) and has sold 2.5 million copies. His success may be attributed to his clarity of communication, his disciplined mind, his passion for mission, his balanced approach, his faithfulness to the Scriptures, his rational persuasiveness, and his sympathetic humanity in his relationships with a worldwide public. His was not an ivory-tower ministry, closeted in his study and confined to his culture of origin, but a risk-taking leadership that ventured beyond the comfort of his home church in the center of London to engage the contemporary world, travel to "the ends of the earth," and enter into the lives of countless Christians of diverse ethnic groups facing unique challenges. His theology proved to be relevant to believers in every continent who cherished his books and assimilated the gospel he taught.

After 53 years of public ministry I find that his words still instruct and inspire me. I have not attempted to systematize his theology but to give "a full and balanced" summary of "his thought and teaching." While many preachers, teachers, and mature disciples may have read one or two of his books, few have the time or opportunity to study the full extent of what Stott believed and taught over his lifetime. By categorizing his thought under separate subjects I hope to provide an accessible resource for busy pastors and teachers, for the benefit of their own lives and to enrich their communication of the gospel. I also hope this will become a useful resource for relevant departments of theological seminaries and Bible and missionary training colleges.

In 1996, evangelical historian Mark Noll considered John Stott "the sanest, clearest and most solidly biblical living writer on theological topics in the English language." Others have considered him one of the most influential Christian figures of the last hundred years. His work endures; and he is read with profit throughout the world. The wisdom that Stott supplies is clear, balanced, reasonable, knowledgeable, practical, compassionate, realistic, and persuasive. He was not just intellectual (although he was intelligent, highly educated, and opposed to anti-intellectualism) but also had understanding of the heart and the experience of ordinary human beings.[4] His output over his life was prodigious; it covered most aspects of the Christian life and the needs of the world. For his readers he provides nourishment for their souls, minds, hearts, relationships, and fodder for their witness and work in the world. If this book is an appetizer, I hope that many will be drawn to the full course in his own writings.

John Stott's conviction was that the gospel of Christ is the only remedy for the ills of civilization. It is a remedy much needed today as we battle fear, pandemics, and economic challenges in addition to the ultimate enemy – death. In every church people are hungry for the bread of life and desperate for meaning and purpose. As Stott wrote about Paul's Letter to the Romans, the fullest and grandest statement of the gospel in the New Testament: "It proclaims freedom from the wrath of God revealed against all ungodliness, freedom from 'the dark little dungeon of our own ego' (Malcolm Muggeridge), freedom from ethnic conflict, freedom from death and the fear of death, freedom from pain and decay in the future redeemed universe, and freedom to live in love for God and our neighbor."[5]

What a gospel to proclaim, to communicate, to live by, and to enjoy! It is the gospel of the Christ in whom Stott believed with all his heart, and in whose service he labored and appealed to others to invite Him into their lives and find for themselves, eternal life.

Ted Schroder, 2021

1

God

While the majority of the world is religious, Communist cultures are atheistic and European and North American ones predominantly secular. This means that the work of Christian pastors, wherever they minister today, must include apologetics, i.e. defending the basic tenets of the Christian faith. The secular educational establishment in traditionally Christian Europe and North America is committed to a scientific worldview that excludes belief in the spiritual or supernatural. Students receive a reductionist view of life that seeks to explain everything in terms of the physical, material, and social environment. The church has the responsibility to provide an alternative view that is based on divine revelation. This will include responding to the big questions of the meaning of life, the purpose of creation, the reason for hope, the basis of human value and significance, and guidance about moral behavior. From the beginning of his ministry, John Stott addressed these issues.

He insisted that we must include apologetics in our evangelism. He wrote that we need to anticipate people's objections to the gospel, listen carefully to their problems, respond to them with due seriousness, and proclaim the gospel in such a way as to affirm God's goodness and further his glory. Such dialogical preaching has powerful apostolic precedent.

Stott presented a threefold argument for the existence of God:

1. *The fact of the universe*. All around us are phenomena that are inexplicable apart from God. He is the Cause from which all effects ultimately derive. He is the Life to which all life owes its being. He is the Energy from which all motion comes. Ps. 19:1; Rom. 1:20; Acts 14:15–17.

2. *The nature of human beings*. Is there some ultimate Beauty, Truth, Goodness and Love to which our whole personality responds? Why are all human beings worshipping creatures, who manufacture their own gods if none is revealed to them?

3. ***The person of Jesus.*** The best and strongest argument for the existence of God is the Jesus of history. If you really want to know God you will get to know Jesus, for he is the image of God, God in the flesh. The Bible assumes the existence of God as Creator and Savior. We cannot know anything about God unless he reveals himself to us. This he does through Nature and through the Scriptures. The opening book of the Bible reveals God as the source of all life.

The *fact* of divine creation is taught in the Bible, and not the *mode*. Many Christians hold to the theory of evolution as an expression of God's creative activity, although it is clearly impossible for a biblical Christian to hold a purely *mechanistic* view of the origin and development of life which virtually dispenses with God. Nor can we regard human beings as nothing but highly evolved animals, for Genesis 1 and 2 affirm the special creation of Adam and Eve in God's image, that is, with a cluster of distinctive faculties (e.g. reason, conscience, will and love) which makes us like God and unlike the animals. Our own self-consciousness strongly confirms this biblical truth. Probably most of us (not least because of the deliberately stylized form of Genesis 1) regard the days as representing stages of creation and would not want to press other details with wooden literalism. ... Science addresses itself to "how" things function; Scripture is preoccupied with "why" questions. The first 3 chapters of Genesis reveal 4 spiritual truths which could never be discovered by the scientific method.

First, that God made everything.

Secondly, that he made it out of nothing. There was no original raw material as eternal as himself on which he could work.

Thirdly, he made man male and female in his image.

Fourthly, that everything which he made was "very good". When it left his hand it was perfect. Sin and suffering were foreign invasions into his lovely world and spoiled it.

God did not leave the world to run on its own like a clockwork toy. God is present and active in it, continually upholding, animating and ordering it and its creatures. Perhaps the dominant theme of the whole Bible is the sovereign, ceaseless, purposeful activity of Almighty God. "Father" is Christianity's distinctive title for God. Jews and Muslims did not address God as Father. There is a distinction between the universal fatherhood of God and the distinctive Fatherhood to Christians (John 1:12; Gal. 3:26; 1 John 3:1). We are dependents of God as our Maker and Sustainer, and as our Father. [*Christian Basics* by John Stott. Copyright ©1991 John R.W. Stott. Reproduced by permission of Hodder & Stoughton][6]

Stott was unrelentingly trinitarian in his understanding of God. Wherever he could, he described God in trinitarian terms. His prayer on arising every morning was trinitarian.

Almighty and everlasting God, Creator and Sustainer of the universe,
I worship you.
Lord Jesus Christ, Savior and Lord of the world,
I worship you.
Holy Spirit, Sanctifier of the people of God,
I worship you.
Glory be to the Father, and to the Son and to the Holy Spirit. As it was in
the beginning is now and ever shall be, world without end. Amen.
Heavenly Father, I pray that
this day I may live in your presence and please you more and more.
Lord Jesus Christ, I pray that
this day I may take up my cross and follow you.
Holy Spirit, I pray that
this day your fruit will ripen my life: love, joy, peace, patience,
kindness, goodness, faithfulness, gentleness and self-control.
Holy, blessed and glorious Trinity, three persons in one God,
have mercy upon me. Amen.[7]

He cites scriptural authority for the trinity in the baptism of Jesus and the Great Commission (Matt. 3:17; 28:19; also 1 Pet. 1:2; 2 Cor. 13:14). He lists three approaches to the truth of the trinity.

First there is the approach of history. It was a gradual unfolding historical revelation. It was the facts of the observation of the apostles about Jesus, his teaching and miracles, and his speaking of God as his Father and the Comforter or Spirit of Truth who would take his place after he left them, which compelled them to believe in the Trinity.

Secondly, there is the approach of theology. The major problem felt by the early church fathers was how they could reconcile the unity of God with both the deity and the distinctness of Jesus, or how they could believe that Jesus was both divine and distinct from the Father without committing themselves to two Gods. All of them began with the unity of God (Deut. 6:4). They failed to define the nature of God's unity. Not mathematical but organic. Within the complex mystery of the infinite God are three eternally distinct personal modes of being.

Thirdly, there is the approach of experience. There are many things in life which we cannot fully explain, but nevertheless experience e.g. electricity, barometric pressure, or love. Every time we pray we enjoy access to the Father through the Son by the Spirit (Eph. 2:18). [*Christian Basics* by John Stott. Copyright ©1991 John R.W. Stott. Reproduced by permission of Hodder & Stoughton][8]

In his commentary on Ephesians, Stott discerned a trinitarian structure.

As we continue to compare the two halves of Ephesians 1, another feature of them strikes us: both are essentially trinitarian. For both are addressed to God the Father, the benediction to "the God and Father of our Lord Jesus Christ" (v.3) and the intercession to "the God of our Lord Jesus Christ" (v.17), who is also called "the Father of glory" or (NEB) "the all-glorious Father". Next, both refer specifically to God's work in and through Christ, for on the one hand he "has blessed us in Christ" (v.3) and on the other he "accomplished in Christ" a mighty act of power when he resurrected and enthroned him (v.20). And thirdly both sections of the chapter allude – even if obliquely – to the work of the Holy Spirit, since the blessings God bestows on us in Christ are "spiritual" blessings (v.3), and it is only "by a spirit (or Spirit) of wisdom and revelation" that we can come to know them (v.17). I do not think it far-fetched to discern this Trinitarian structure. Christian faith and Christian life are both fundamentally trinitarian. And the one is a response to the other. It is because the Father has approached us in blessing through the Son and by the Spirit that we approach him in prayer through the Son and by the Spirit also (cf. 2:18).[9]

In the Lord's Prayer he saw a trinitarian exposition: "a trinitarian Christian is bound to see in these three petitions a veiled allusion to the three persons of the Trinity, since it is through the Father's creation and providence that we receive our daily bread through the Son's atoning death that we receive the forgiveness of our sins, and through the Holy Spirit's indwelling power that we can be rescued from the evil one."[10]

God is seen to be holy, i.e. separate from sinful humanity. God cannot coexist with sin. We cannot approach God in our own merit, and God cannot tolerate our sin. Therefore we, as sinners, must have a healthy respect for God and not an overly familiar attitude.

Several vivid metaphors are used in Scripture to illustrate this stubborn fact.

The first is *height*. Frequently in the Bible the god of creation and covenant is called "the Most High God." His lofty exaltation expresses both his sovereignty over the nations, the earth and "all gods," and also his inaccessibility to sinners.

The second picture is that of *distance*. God is not only "high above" us, but "far away" from us also. We dare not approach too close. Indeed, many are the biblical injunctions to keep our distance.

The third and fourth pictures of the holy God's unapproachability to sinners are those of *light* and *fire*. "God is light," and "our God is a consuming fire." Both discourage, indeed inhibit, too close an approach. Bright light is blinding; our eyes cannot endure its brilliance, and in the heat of the fire everything shrivels up and is destroyed.

The fifth metaphor is the most dramatic of all. It indicates that the holy God's rejection of evil is as decisive as the human body's rejection of poison by *vomiting*. Vomiting is probably the body's most violent of all reactions. The immoral and idolatrous practices of the Canaanites were so disgusting, it is written "the land vomited out its inhabitants." God cannot tolerate or "digest" sin and hypocrisy. They cause him not distaste merely, but disgust. They are so repulsive to him that he must rid himself of them. He must spit or vomit them out.

All five metaphors illustrate the utter incompatibility of divine holiness and human sin. Height and distance, light, fire and vomiting all say that God cannot be in the presence of sin, and that if it approaches him too closely it is repudiated or consumed.

Yet these notions are foreign to common man. The kind of God who appeals to most people today would be easygoing in his tolerance of our offences. He would be gentle, kind, accommodating, and would have no violent reactions. Unhappily, even in the church we seem to have lost the vision of the majesty of God. There is much shallowness and levity among us. Prophets and psalmists would probably say of us that "there is no fear of God before their eyes." In public worship our habit is to slouch or squat; we do not kneel nowadays, let alone prostrate ourselves in humility before God. It is more characteristic of us to clap our hands with joy than to blush with shame or tears. We saunter up to God to claim his patronage and friendship; it does not occur to us that he might send us away. ...

We must, therefore, hold fast to the biblical revelation of the living God who hates evil, is disgusted and angered by it, and refuses ever to come to terms with it. ... As Emil Brunner put it, "Where the idea of the wrath of God is ignored, there also will be no understanding of the central conception of the Gospel: the uniqueness of the revelation in the Mediator." Similarly, "only he who knows the greatness of wrath will be mastered by the greatness of mercy."

When we have glimpsed the blinding glory of the holiness of God, and have been so convicted of our sin by the Holy Spirit that we tremble before God, and acknowledge what we are, namely, "hell-deserving sinners," then and only then does the necessity of the cross appear so obvious that we are astonished we never saw it before.

The essential background to the cross, therefore, is a balanced understanding of the gravity of sin and the majesty of God. If we diminish either, we thereby diminish the cross. If we reinterpret sin as a lapse instead of a rebellion, and God as indulgent instead of indignant, then naturally the cross appears superfluous. But to dethrone God and enthrone ourselves not only dispenses with the cross; it also degrades both God and man. A biblical view of God and ourselves, however, that is of our sin and of God's wrath, honors both. It honors human beings by affirming them as responsible for their own actions. It honors God by affirming him as having moral character.[11]

The proper attitude to God is holy reverence, which in the Bible is called "the fear of the Lord." Mary, in the Magnificat, is an example of such an attitude.

The Bible says much about "the fear of the Lord". We are told in the Psalms, in the book of Job, and in the Proverbs that "the fear of the Lord is the beginning of wisdom". Part of the indictment of the heathen world is that "there is no fear of God before their eyes". Jesus told us, "Fear him who can destroy both body and soul in hell", referring to his Father in heaven; and the early disciples are described as "walking in the fear of the Lord".

There is too much shallow frivolity and irreverence in the world, and even in the Church, today. Men have pried open so many locked secrets that there is little left which they regard as sacred. Even in religious circles many people seem to be characterized by an inane bonhomie which has neither depth nor substance. People have so lost sight of the unfathomable majesty of God, that they have tended to become over-familiar with him. They imagine that they can link arms with him as if he were their partner on the golf course.

Such people God scatters in the imaginations of their hearts. His mercy is rather on those who fear him. The Virgin Mary was a simple, devout, God-fearing maiden; we must follow her example if we hope to share her experience.[12]

2

Christ

John Stott believed and taught that Christ is the center of Christianity. Stott's best-selling book, *Basic Christianity*, is an exposition of who Christ is, what Christ has done, and how a seeker should respond to him. He begins with the claims of Christ.

> The crucial issue is this: was the carpenter of Nazareth the Son of God? The great question in Christianity remains: what do you think of Christ? ... Essentially Christianity is Christ. The person and work of Christ are the foundation rock upon which the Christian religion is built. If he is not who he said he was, and if he did not do what he said he had come to do, the whole superstructure of Christianity crumbles to the ground. Take Christ from Christianity, and you disembowel it; there is practically nothing left. Christ is the center of Christianity; all else is circumference. We are not concerned primarily to discuss the nature of his philosophy, the value of his system, or the quality of his ethics. Our concern is fundamentally with the character of his person.
>
> ... Our purpose is to marshal evidence to prove that Jesus was the only begotten Son of God. ... We believe him to possess an eternal and essential relation to God possessed by no other person. We regard him neither as God in human disguise, nor as a man with divine qualities; we believe him to be God made man. We are persuaded that Jesus was a historic person possessing two distinct and perfect natures, Godhead and manhood, and in this to be absolutely and for ever unique. Only so could he be worthy not just of our admiration but of our worship.
>
> ... The evidence is threefold. It concerns the claims Christ made, his moral character and his resurrection from the dead.[13]

What follows is an exhaustive presentation of evidence from the New Testament.

First, *the egocentric character of Christ's teaching* – he referred to himself as the "bread of life," the "light of the world," the "resurrection and the life," the "way, the truth and the life," the "true vine," and the "living water."

Secondly, he made *direct claims* to be the Messiah, the Son of Man, the great "I AM" of God revealed before Abraham and Moses, and worthy of the designation "My Lord and my God" from Thomas.

Thirdly, he *indirectly claimed* to forgive sins, to bestow life, to teach the truth with divine authority, and to judge the world when he returns in glory.

Fourthly, his miracles were *dramatized claims* illustrating his moral authority.

Stott goes on to explore the character of Jesus. "Was he a deliberate impostor? Did he attempt to gain the adherence of men to his views by assuming a divine authority he did not possess? ... Was he sincerely mistaken. We need not call him mad; but had he a fixed delusion about himself. ... Jesus does not give the impression of that abnormality one expects to find in the deluded."[14]

He concentrates on the sinlessness of Christ, as shown by his own self-aware-ness of his moral purity and by the views of his disciples. Stott concludes Jesus was the most unselfish man who ever lived.

> Above all, he was unselfish. Nothing is more striking than this. Believing himself to be divine, he yet did not put on airs or stand on his dignity. He was never pompous as men tend to be who think themselves greater than they are. There was no touch of self-importance about Jesus. He was humble. It is this paradox which is so baffling, the self-centeredness of his teaching and the unself-centeredness of his behavior. In thought he put himself first; in deed last. He combined in himself the greatest self-esteem and the greatest self-sacrifice. ... His renunciations are tremendous. It is claimed (by him as well as by us) that he renounced the joys of heaven for the sorrows of earth, exchanging an eternal immunity to the approach of sin for painful contact with evil in this world. He was born of a lowly Hebrew mother in a dirty stable in the insignificant village of Bethlehem. He became a refugee baby in Egypt. He was brought up in the obscure hamlet of Nazareth, and toiled at a carpenter's bench to support his mother and the other children in their home. In due time he became an itinerant preacher, with few possessions, small comforts and no home. He made friends with simple fishermen and publicans. He touched lepers and allowed harlots to touch him. He gave himself away in a ministry of healing, helping, teaching and preaching.
>
> He was misunderstood and misrepresented and became the victim of men's prejudices and vested interests. He was despised and gave his back to be flogged, his face to be spat upon, his head to be crowned with thorns,

his hands and feet to be nailed to a common Roman gallows. And as the cruel spikes were driven home, he kept praying for his tormentors, "Father, forgive them; for they know not what they do."

Such a man is altogether beyond our reach. He succeeded just where we invariably fail. He has complete self-mastery. He never retaliated. He never grew resentful or irritable. He has such control of himself that, whatever men might think or say or do, he would deny himself and abandon himself to the will of God and the welfare of mankind. "I seek not my own will," he said, and "I do not seek my own glory." As Paul wrote, "For Christ did not please himself."

This utter disregard of self in the service of God and man is what the Bible calls love.[15]

In *The Authentic Jesus: a response to current scepticism in the church*, published in 1985, he defended the uniqueness of Jesus. He argued that the man Christ Jesus is also God. Not a man with divine qualities, nor God appearing in human disguise, but God the eternal Son (or Word) who actually "became flesh" (John 1:14). He cited the four great Ecumenical Councils of the fourth and fifth centuries, concluding with a summary of the Chalcedonian Definition of 451: "One and the selfsame Son, our Lord, is perfect in godhead, perfect in manhood, begotten of the Father eternally as to divinity, but born of the virgin temporally as to humanity. There is one Christ in two natures, unconfusedly, unchangeably, indivisibly and inseparably."[16]

The Reformers endorsed these statements of the early church. The second Anglican Article of Religion (1563) reads: "The Son, who is the Word of the Father, begotten from everlasting of the Father ... took Man's nature in the womb of the blessed Virgin, of her substance: so that two whole and perfect Natures, that is to say, the Godhead and Manhood, were joined together in one Person, never to be divided, whereof is one Christ, very God, and very Man." This, Stott states, is the foundation of the New Testament documents.

There are three claims of Jesus that Stott repeated constantly.

First, Jesus claimed that *he was the fulfillment of all Old Testament prophecy* (Matt. 13:16,17).

Secondly, he claimed *to enjoy in his relationship with the Father an intimacy that was shared by nobody else* (Matt. 11:27).

Thirdly, he claimed *to have authority over all people to teach them about God, to call them to himself, to forgive their sins, and to judge them on the last day.*

The early Christians gave Jesus the Old Testament title of LORD, for God, and transferred to Jesus Old Testament God-texts (e.g. Isa. 45:23; Phil. 2:9–11; Joel 2:32; Rom. 10:9–13). This transfer identifies Jesus as God – able to save and worthy of worship. "Nobody can call himself a Christian who does not worship Jesus. To worship him, if he is not God, is idolatry; to withhold worship from him, if he is, is apostasy."[17]

The uniqueness of Christ lies in his birth, death, and resurrection. The Father gave to the world in and through his incarnate Son a unique historical revelation of himself. The Incarnation was a historical and unrepeatable event with permanent consequences. Reigning at God's right hand today is the man Christ Jesus, still human as well as divine, though now his humanity has been glorified. Having assumed our human nature, he has never discarded it, and he never will. God in Christ took our place on the cross, bore our sins, suffered our penalty, and died our death, in order that we might be forgiven, reconciled and recreated. There is nothing even approaching this in other religions. The resurrection is unique. By it God vindicated Jesus, defeated death and inaugurated his new creation. In addition, Jesus' resurrection from death was the prelude to, even the beginning of, his exaltation as Lord. The Spirit glorifies Christ and makes him available to everybody everywhere (John 16:7). The Spirit makes Christ's indwelling within us a personal reality (John 14:17f.).

In no other person but the historic Jesus of Nazareth has God become man and lived a human life on earth, died to bear the penalty of our sins, been raised from death and exalted to glory; there is no other Savior, for there is no other person who is qualified to save (Acts 4:12).[18]

In 1978 John Stott preached a series of sermons in All Souls Church, London that was published the following year under the title, *Focus on Christ: an enquiry into the theology of prepositions.*

> My theme in this little book is that Jesus Christ is the center of Christianity, and that therefore both the Christian faith and the Christian life, if they are to be authentic, must be 'focused on Christ'. … My concern is to examine the implications of a Christian faith and life which are focused on Christ, and to do so by means of the prepositions which are used in the New Testament in reference to him. This is why I have sub-titled the book 'an enquiry into the theology of prepositions.[19]

His chapters are headed:

1. Through Christ our Mediator

2. On Christ our Foundation

3. In Christ our Life-Giver

4. Under Christ our Lord

5. With Christ our Secret

6. Unto Christ our Goal

7. For Christ our Lover

8. Like Christ our Model

First, Stott argues, "whatever we know of God we know through Jesus Christ, and whatever we have received from God we have received through Jesus Christ." Christ mediates our relationship with God.

Secondly, Jesus is the "ground on which we stand, the support on which we rely or the foundation on which we build." We rest on the work of Christ, we rely on the promises of Christ and we build on the teaching of Christ. There is no other foundation than that laid, which is Jesus Christ.

Thirdly, to be in Christ is to be united to him in a very close personal relationship. "Remain in me, as I also remain in you" (John 15:4,5). To be a Christian is primarily to live in union with Jesus Christ.

Fourthly, we have the mind of Christ because we have put ourselves under the yoke of Christ. We put our wills under the yoke of Christ because we acknowledge his authority as our Lord and we wish to obey his commands (Matt. 11:29,30).

Fifthly, we have died with Christ, we have been raised with Christ, our life is hidden with Christ, and we shall appear with Christ. The essence of our Christian identity is that we are "with Christ" at each stage of his saving career.

Sixthly, we are to set Christ always before us, to keep him constantly in our minds and before our eyes. Our life is directed towards him. Our ambition is to please, to serve, and to obey him, and our supreme concern is that in all things he may be glorified. The greatest need is to see Christ in every situation and every relationship. We shall see him in or behind others and, seeing him, shall treat them as we would treat him.

Seventhly, our motive is to live and work "for Christ," for his sake. We live no longer for ourselves but for him who for our sake died and was raised (2 Cor. 5:14,15).

Eighthly, we are to become like Christ through the inward work of the Holy Spirit (2 Cor. 3:18).

In his Cornerstone column for *Christianity Today* on 12 June 1981, John Stott wrote about the deity of Christ and the gravity of "allowing flagrant Unitarian heresy to be unanswered, unchecked, and undisciplined in the church."[20] The central issue for him was salvation (whether Jesus can in any sense mediate between God and mankind if he is not himself both God and man) and of discipleship (for we cannot worship him, believe in him, or obey him if he is not God). He goes on to write "by the middle of the first century, the deity of Jesus was part of the faith of the universal church. It cannot and must not be compromised today."

In 2000 Stott gave the London Lectures in Contemporary Christianity on "Jesus." All Souls Church in London was nearly full for each of the lectures. They attracted a distinguished audience. Princess Alexandra attended the last lecture and Stott was introduced by George Carey, the Archbishop of Canterbury. The following year the expanded lectures were published as *The Incomparable Christ*. Stott's concern was to ask and answer four basic questions about Christ. (1) How does the New Testament bear witness to him? (2) How has the church portrayed Jesus Christ down the centuries? (3) What influence has Christ had in history? (4) What should Jesus Christ mean to us today?

In Part I: ***The Original Jesus***, he surveyed the New Testament witness and identified the central theme of each section of it. For the Gospel of Matthew, he saw Christ portrayed as the fulfillment of Scripture. The Gospel of Mark portrays Christ as the Suffering Servant. Luke's Gospel and Acts portray Christ as the Savior of the world. The Gospel and letters of John portray Christ as the Word made flesh. Galatians portrays Christ as the liberator; Thessalonians as Christ the coming Judge; Romans and Corinthians as Christ the Savior; Ephesians, Colossians, Philemon and Philippians as Christ the supreme Lord; Timothy and Titus as Christ the Head of the church; James as Christ the moral Teacher; Hebrews as Christ our great High Priest; the letters of Peter as Christ the exemplary Sufferer.

In Part II: ***The Ecclesiastical Jesus***, Stott used representative teachers as examples of how the church has presented Jesus. Justin Martyr presents Jesus as the complete fulfillment of the promises of the Old Testament prophets and the embodiment of all that is best in Greek philosophy. The early councils of the church witnessed to the complete understanding of the unique Christ as both true God and true man. St. Benedict presented Jesus as the perfect monk, which caused Stott to question whether aspects of monasticism were setting up first-class and second-class Christians. Anselm presented Christ as the feudal debtor in his atonement theology. Bernard of Clairvaux presented Christ as the heavenly bridegroom, which led Stott to question the nature of Christian mysticism and the use of allegory. Thomas à Kempis presented Jesus as the ethical exemplar in *The Imitation of Christ*, but erred into legalism and asceticism, and neglected the gospel of grace. Martin Luther presented Jesus as the gracious Savior who justified us by his grace through faith. Ernst Renan and Thomas Jefferson portrayed Jesus as a moral teacher, but not as divine. John Mackay, Presbyterian missionary in Lima, Peru and afterwards President of Princeton Theological Seminary, criticized the Spanish Catholicism introduced into South America that presented Jesus as tragic victim, the center of a cult of suffering and death, ever on the cross but never resurrected. Gustavo Gutierrez in his liberation theology presented Jesus as the social liberator, champion of the poor and the oppressed. N.T. Wright, Anglican theologian, reconstructed Christ as the Jewish Messiah. Finally, Stott reviewed the history of the missionary movement of the twentieth century, culminating in the Lausanne Covenant that clarified the uniqueness and universality of Christ in the face of pluralism and syncretism.

In Part III: *The Influential Jesus*, he gave twelve examples of how Jesus has inspired people to give their lives to the service of others and to bring about social reform. From Francis of Assisi to William Wilberforce, he told the stories of how Jesus and his message affected key lives.

In Part IV: *The Eternal Jesus*, he surveyed how the book of Revelation portrays Jesus as our contemporary, confronting every new generation, century, and millennium in his roles of Savior, Lord, and Judge.

Stott concluded his lectures by warning the readers to avoid portraying Jesus in their own image and bearing little resemblance to the authentic Jesus of apostolic witness. The only way to come to know the authentic Jesus for ourselves is to kneel in humility before his depiction in the Scriptures.

3

The Holy Spirit

Stott summarized the teaching of the apostles about the Holy Spirit. While he came upon them at Pentecost, as promised by Jesus, the Spirit was active and existing before all time. He is the divine, eternal Spirit who has been at work in the world since creation. "In the beginning, God created the heavens and the earth ... and the Spirit of God was hovering over the waters" (Gen. 1:1,2). The Old Testament bears witness to him; the prophets looked forward to his increasing activity.

> Ezekiel and Jeremiah in particular spoke of his future work within God's people. "A new heart I will give you, and a new spirit I will put within you; and I will take out of your flesh the heart of stone and give you a heart of flesh. And I will put my spirit within you, and cause you to walk in my statutes and be careful to observe my ordinances." Here the gift of a new heart is closely linked with the indwelling of God's Spirit, and the result will be a life of obedience to his law. Jeremiah's wonderful prophecy of a new covenant includes a similar provision, "I will put my law within them, and I will write it upon their hearts" (Ezek. 36:26,27; Jer. 31:33). The people of God will no longer have an external code engraved on stone tablets which they cannot obey, but the law of God written in their hearts by the Holy Spirit, who will not only teach it to them but give them power to conform their lives to its requirements. What the Old Testament prophets foretold about seven hundred years before Christ, Christ promised as an immediate expectation (John 16:7; 14:17). ... When we put our trust in Jesus Christ and commit ourselves to him, the Holy Spirit enters us. He is sent by God into our hearts. He makes our bodies his temple (Gal. 4:6; 1 Cor. 6:19).[21]

The work of the Holy Spirit is to universalize and to internalize the presence of Jesus. The bodily presence of Jesus was succeeded by the Holy Spirit being always with us, wherever we may be, and entering into our personalities to change us into his image from within. The Holy Spirit is the "executive" of the Godhead, meaning that what the Father and the Son desire to do in the world today, they execute through the Holy Spirit. Stott listed seven areas of the Spirit's ministry, which I abbreviate as follows:

1. *Christian conversion.* He begins by convicting or convincing the world of sin, righteousness and judgment (John 16:8–10). "Every stab of conscience and pang of guilt, every sense of alienation and longing for reconciliation, and every anxious fear of coming judgment are prompted by him. Next, he opens our eyes to see the truth, glory and saving power of Jesus ... The Holy Spirit moves us to repent and believe, and so to experience the new birth. For to be born again is to be 'born of the Spirit' (John 3:6–8)."[22] The Nicene Creed rightly calls him "the Lord, the Giver of life."

2. *Christian assurance.* The Holy Spirit is God's "seal" to indicate that we are now his own (2 Cor. 1:22; Eph. 1:13; 4:30). The indwelling Spirit actively assures us of God's love and fatherhood (Rom. 5:5; 8:16). He is the guarantee or down-payment of our future inheritance (2 Cor. 1:22; Eph. 1:14).

3. *Christian holiness.* "His ministry is not only to show Christ to us, but also to form Christ in us. And he does it by penetrating deeply into the hidden recesses of our personality. We are to live by the Spirit, be led by the Spirit, and keep in step with the Spirit, surrendering daily to his mastery and following his promptings" (Gal. 5:16,18,25).

4. *Christian understanding.* He is the Spirit of truth (John 14:17; 15:26; 16:13). He believes, loves, defends, and teaches the truth. He is the primary author of Scripture and its primary interpreter. He spoke through the prophets in the Old Testament and the apostles in the New Testament. "He will teach you all things. ... he will guide you into all the truth" (John 15:26; 16:13). We need his illumination to understand and to apply the word of God in the Scriptures to our lives.

5. *Christian fellowship.* What happened at Pentecost was that the remnant of God's people became the Spirit-filled body of Christ. The church is the fellowship of the Holy Spirit. "There is one body and one Spirit" (Eph. 4:4). We are united by the Spirit.

6. *Christian service.* The Spirit gives both supernatural and natural abilities to members of the church. The gifts of the Spirit are for service to be used for the common good, so that the church is built up and grows into maturity. We should emphasize the teaching gifts, since nothing nurtures the church like the truth. The love of Christ is the supreme gift.

7. *Christian mission.* It is the Spirit who empowers us to witness to Christ. There is perhaps no greater need in the contemporary church than for

believers to be filled with the Holy Spirit (Eph. 5:18). "We need him not only to bring us to conversion and assurance, nor only to sanctify, enlighten, unite and equip us, but also to reach out through us in blessing to an alienated world, like rivers of living water which irrigate the desert (John 7:38,39)."[23] [*Christian Basics* by John Stott. Copyright ©1991 John R.W. Stott. Reproduced by permission of Hodder & Stoughton]

On 7 January 1964 Stott spoke at the Islington Clerical Conference in London on the controversial subject of "The Baptism and Fullness of the Holy Spirit." His address was expanded and published later that year under the same title. He confronted the "recrudescence of 'Pentecostalism' in non-Pentecostal churches, which rejoices some and bewilders or even alarms others. Christians of some years' standing are claiming to have received a 'baptism' of (or in) the Spirit and to give evidence of it by 'signs following.'"[24] The most prominent sign was that of speaking in tongues. One of Stott's own staff members, Michael Harper, claimed this had happened to him. This caused friction between them and led to Harper's leaving All Souls in 1964 to found the Fountain Trust, which promoted charismatic renewal in all churches.

Stott began by arguing that the full purpose of God is to be discerned in Scripture, not in the experience of particular individuals or groups, however true and valid these experiences may be. The *didactic* parts of Scripture should govern our understanding not the *historical* parts. The purpose of God should be sought in the teaching of Jesus, and in the sermons and writings of the apostles, and not in the purely narrative portions of the Acts. "What is described in Scripture as having happened to others is not necessarily intended for us, whereas what is promised to us we are to appropriate, and what is commanded us we are to obey."[25] He went on to elaborate three major propositions about the individual Christian and the fullness of the Holy Spirit.

First, *the fullness of the Holy Spirit is one of the distinctive blessings of the new age*. The "new age" is "the dispensation of the Spirit" (2 Cor. 3:8; Acts 2:38; Titus 3:4–7). When we repent and believe, Jesus not only takes away our sins but also baptizes us with the Holy Spirit. "[T]hese are the two great gifts of Jesus Christ our Savior." Salvation includes the positive blessing of an indwelling Spirit.

Secondly, *the fullness of the Holy Spirit is not only a distinctive blessing of the new age, but a universal blessing* (Acts 2:39). This means that, according to Acts 2, two separate companies of people received the "baptism" or "gift" of the Spirit on the day of Pentecost – the 120 at the beginning of the chapter, and the 3,000 at the end. The three thousand do not seem to have experienced the same miraculous phenomena (the rushing mighty wind, the tongues of flame, or speaking in other tongues). Yet they inherited the same promise and received the same gift (vv.33,39). Nevertheless, there was then a difference between them: the 120 were regenerate already, and only received the baptism of the Spirit after waiting upon God for ten days. The 3,000, on the other hand were unbelievers, and received the forgiveness of their sins and the gift of the Spirit simultaneously – and that immediately they repented and believed, without any necessity to wait. This distinction between the two companies, the 120 and the 3,000, is of great importance, because, Stott suggested, that the norm for Christian experience today is the second group, the 3,000, and not (as is often supposed) the first. "What the general teaching of the New Testament is regarding the reception of the Holy Spirit, we can give a plain and definite answer: we receive the Holy Spirit 'by hearing [the gospel] with faith' (Gal. 3:2) or, more simply still, 'through faith' (Gal. 3:14). As a result all God's sons possess the Spirit (Gal. 4:6), and are led by the Spirit (Rom. 8:14), and are assured by the Spirit of their sonship and of God's love (Rom. 8:15,16; 5:5)."[26]

After reviewing the incidents of the disciples of John the Baptist in Ephesus (Acts 19:1–7) and the Samaritan believers in Acts 8:5–17, Stott concluded that they were untypical. "The very concept of 'baptism' is initiatory. Water-baptism is the rite of initiation into Christ. It is the symbol of which Spirit-baptism is the reality. 'For by one Spirit we were all baptized into one body' (1 Cor. 12:13). ... The oneness of the body is created by the oneness of the Spirit (Eph. 4:3,4). It is difficult to resist the conclusion that the baptism of the Spirit is not a second and subsequent experience, enjoyed by some Christians, but the initial experience enjoyed by all."[27]

Thirdly, *the fullness of the Holy Spirit, is also a continuous blessing*, to be continuously and increasingly appropriated (John 7:37–39). If this is so, why is it that many Christians live on a level lower than their Spirit-baptism makes possible? It is because they do not remain filled with the Holy Spirit.

They need to recover the fullness of the Spirit which they have lost through sin, thus becoming what the Corinthian Christians were, namely "unspiritual" or "carnal" (1 Cor. 3:1ff.). The result of the baptism of the Spirit is that "they were all filled with the Holy Spirit" (Acts 2:4). The fullness of the Spirit was the consequence of the baptism of the Spirit. This fullness was intended to be the continuing, the permanent result, the norm. As an initiatory event, the baptism was not repeatable, and could not be lost, but the filling can be repeated, and needed to be maintained. If it is not maintained, it is lost. If it is lost, it can be recovered. The Holy Spirit is "grieved" by sin (Eph. 4:30) and ceases to fill the sinner. Repentance is then the only road to recovery. Even in cases where there is no suggestion that the fullness has been forfeited through sin, we still read of people being filled again, as a fresh crisis or challenge demands a fresh empowering by the Spirit (Acts 4:8,31; 9:17; 13:9). Ephesians 5:18 contains the well-known command to all Christian people to be filled, that is, to go on being filled with the Spirit.[28]

Stott concluded that the Pentecostal teaching that "speaking in tongues" is the indispensable sign of having received the Spirit, cannot be maintained from Scripture. The apostle teaches in 1 Corinthians 12 that the gift of tongues is only one of many gifts, which not all are given to every believer.

What then is evidence of the Spirit's indwelling and fullness? The chief evidence is moral not miraculous; it consists of the fruit of the Spirit not the gifts of the Spirit:

The first sign of fullness is *fellowship in common worship*.

The second result is glorifying the Lord Jesus in *singing and making melody*.

Thirdly, it leads to *thanksgiving* for all things (Eph. 5:18; Col. 3:16).

Stott acknowledged that the Holy Spirit can work abnormally in some believers.

> There are unusual, special operations of the Holy Spirit, notably perhaps in times of revival. Sometimes the bestowing of certain spiritual gifts seems to be accompanied by a quickening, an enriching, a deepening of the recipient's spiritual life. Sometimes a fresh filling with the Holy Spirit, especially after a period of disobedience and declension, may lift the penitent believer suddenly on to an altogether new plane of spiritual life and power. Sometimes the Holy Spirit's inward witness to the believer may be strongly and wonderfully confirmed in his heart, so that he is completely delivered from doubt and darkness. Sometimes the Holy Spirit may come upon a believer to intensify his Christian life in what might be called a personal revival or visitation. Sometimes a Christian worker is given supernatural power for the particular work to which God has called him. ... Sometimes the Holy Spirit may even be given to the believer what he gave to the apostle Paul, "visions and revelations of the Lord," so that Paul said he was "caught up to the third heaven" and "heard things which cannot be told, which man may not utter" (1 Cor. 12:1–4) ... Nevertheless, these are not the usual, general, or common purpose of God for all his people, but the unusual, particular, and exceptional ministries of the Holy Spirit to some. Those to whom the sovereign Spirit grants such experiences should indeed bow down and worship God with gratitude. But they should not, if they are true to Scripture, refer to any of them as the baptism of the Spirit. Nor

should they urge the same experiences upon others as if it were the spiritual norm. Nor should they suggest that such unusual spiritual experiences are the secret of either holiness or usefulness, since many in the history of the Church have been powerful in character and ministry without them.[29]

Stott himself prayed for the filling of the Holy Spirit every day.

After the Christmas Day services in 1970 he flew from London to attend the Inter-Varsity student missions conference held at Urbana, Illinois. He was slated to give the four daily Bible readings to the 12,300 conventioneers from 48 states and 72 countries. His subject was the Upper Room Discourse (John 13–17). The expositions were published in 1971, with the addresses of the other speakers, as *Christ the Liberator*. In his second exposition he highlighted four paragraphs about the ministry of the Holy Spirit in John 14–16.

1. *The Spirit will recall Christ's teaching* (14:25,26). He will "remind you of everything I have said to you." This promise was addressed first and foremost to the apostles. The "you" whom the Spirit will remind of Christ's teaching are the "you" to whom Christ has spoken while he was still with them. The fulfilment of this great promise is to be seen in the writing of the New Testament, and in particular of the Gospels. We owe the Gospels ultimately to the work of the Holy Spirit in recalling what had taken place to the mind and memory of the original hearers and, indeed, interpreting it to them.

2. *The Spirit will bear witness to Christ* (15:26,27). "But the Advocate, the Holy Spirit, whom the Father will send in my name, will teach you all things and will remind you of everything I have said to you." Stott explains: "The Holy Spirit's purpose in recalling Christ's teaching to them was not that they should guard it like some priceless treasure for themselves, but that they should share it with the world. The Gospels are not biography; they are testimony."[30]

3. *The Spirit will convict of sin, righteousness and judgment* (16:8-11). "When he comes, he will prove the world to be in the wrong about sin and righteousness and judgment."

   This is another aspect of the Spirit's ministry – to the world rather than to the church, that is, to unbelievers not believers. It is also portrayed in legal terms. The Spirit is securing a conviction. He convinces or convicts the world of three things: the gravity of sin, the possibility of righteousness, and the certainty of judgment. In each case he brings forth evidence by which to secure the conviction. The Spirit convinces the world of sin. Jesus said, "because they do not believe in me" (v.9). Jesus Christ is light come into the world, but men love darkness rather than light. As Tasker comments, "The root of sin lies in the desire of men to live their lives in self-centeredness independence disowning any allegiance to Jesus." [See endnote 31.]

The Spirit convinces the world of righteousness, Jesus said, "because I go to the Father and you will see me no more" (v.10). The departure of Jesus to the Father would be by his resurrection and ascension. These would vindicate his sin-bearing death as a finished and satisfactory work, and so convince men that righteousness can be theirs through Christ.

The Spirit convinces the world of judgment, Jesus said, "because the ruler of the world is judged" (v.11). He would win a victory over the devil. If therefore the ruler of this world had been judged, the world he rules will one day be judged also.

So it is, Jesus taught, that the Holy Spirit uses men's unbelief to prove the gravity of their sin, Christ's triumph to prove the possibility of their righteousness, and the devil's overthrow to prove the certainty of their judgment. The fact of sin and the solemn alternatives of righteousness or judgment become vital realities only when the Holy Spirit is doing his convicting work.[31]

4. **The Spirit will lead into all truth** (16:12–15). "I have much more to say to you, more than you can now bear. But when he, the Spirit of truth, comes, he will guide you into all the truth. He will not speak on his own; he will speak only what he hears, and he will tell you what is yet to come. He will glorify me because it is from me that he will receive what he will make known to you. All that belongs to the Father is mine. That is why I said the Spirit will receive from me what he will make known to you."

It is essential to see that the primary reference is to the apostles. For this promise has been misapplied both by Catholics and liberal Protestants.

The Catholic applies it to the *church* and claims that, as the spirit teaches the church, the church's teaching has supreme authority. The liberal Protestant applies it to the *individual* and claims that as the Spirit teaches the individual, his own reason has supreme authority. But the evangelical applies it to the apostles and claims that, as the Spirit inspired the *apostles*, it is their teaching (in the New Testament) which has supreme authority.

In other words, the Spirit's ministry to the apostles would be both a reminding and a supplementing ministry. He would remind them of what Christ had said to them and supplement it with what Christ had not been able to say. Both promises were fulfilled in the writing of the New Testament, the Gospels being the product of the Spirit's reminding ministry and the epistles the product of the Spirit's supplementing ministry.

This is not to say that the Holy Spirit has been idle in the subsequent post-apostolic history of the church, but rather that his ministry has changed. He was leading the apostles into all the truth; he has been leading the church into an understanding of the truth into which he led the apostles. His work through the apostles was one of revelation; his work in the church is one of illumination, enlightening our minds to grasp what he has revealed.

Here then is the wider ministry of the Holy Spirit, continuing, extending and applying the ministry of Christ. It is a fourfold work, and the Lord Jesus Christ himself is central to each aspect of it. Whether the Spirit is working with Christians or non-Christians, with the church or the world, his is a Christ-centered ministry.

First, he reminded the apostles of all Christ's earthly teaching. Then he supplemented and completed it, leading them into all the truth, revealing Christ to them in all his fullness. Thirdly, through the resulting teaching of the apostles (now preserved in the New Testament) the Spirit has ever since been convicting the world of sin, righteousness and judgment in relation to Christ. Fourthly, through the same unique apostolic testimony, faithfully expounded and personally attested by subsequent generations, the Spirit has been bearing witness to Christ.

The work of the Spirit can never be considered apart from Jesus Christ. He is the Spirit of Christ. His paramount concern is to reveal Christ to us and to form Christ in us.[32]

4

Humanity

John Stott liked to quote Charles Simeon, Vicar of Holy Trinity, Cambridge. In a letter dated July 1825 Simeon writes, "The truth is not in the middle, and not in one extreme, but in both extremes. ... Sometimes I am a high Calvinist, and at other times a low Arminian, so that if extremes will please you, I am your man; only remember, it is not one extreme that we are to go to, but both extremes." Stott goes on to comment, "Thus Charles Simeon would warn us against adopting either one or other extreme or even the golden mean of Aristotle. He would have us hold fast to both extremes, so long as they are equally biblical, even if our human mind cannot reconcile or systematize them. For biblical truth is often stated paradoxically and the attempt to resolve all the 'antinomies' of Scripture is misguided because impossible."[33]

Nowhere is this advice more pertinent than in Stott's theology of humanity. He had a high view of human dignity and worth, and also a low view of human sinfulness and depravity. Both extremes are to be kept in mind because both are biblical. He holds to Jesus as his authority and asks the question: what did Jesus think and say about human nature? I abbreviate his answer as follows:

> The first thing to be said is that he taught the essential dignity of man. Although he is never recorded as having used the expression, there is no doubt that he accepted the Old Testament assertion that God made man in his own image, endowing him with capacities – rational, moral, social and spiritual – which distinguish him from animals. And despite man's fallenness and sinfulness (to which we shall come in a moment), Jesus evidently thought of him as still retaining vestiges of his former glory. So he spoke of man's value. Man is of more value than a sheep, he said; of much more value than many sparrows (Matt. 12:12; 10:31). And the clearest evidence he gave of the value he placed on man was his own mission, which was undertaken solely for man's benefit. Like a shepherd who, having lost a single sheep, first misses it and then braves hardship and danger to rescue it, so God misses human beings who get lost and sent Jesus Christ as the Good Shepherd to seek and to save them. Further, his search for straying

sheep would take him to the cross. "The good shepherd lays down his life for the sheep" (John 10:11). Nothing reveals more clearly the precious-ness of men to God and the love of God for men than the death of God's Son for their salvation. As William Temple put it, "My worth is what I am worth to God, and that is a marvelous good deal, for Christ died for me."

Nevertheless, side by side with his teaching on the essential dignity of man Christ affirmed man's actual degradation. The Old Testament had taught that "there is none that does good, no, not one" (Psalm 14:3); Jesus took over this doctrine and endorsed it. Two or three times he referred to his contemporaries as an "evil and adulterous generation" (Matt. 12:39; Mark 8:38) – "evil" because of their unbelief and disobedience, "adulter-ous" because they had transferred their love and loyalty from the living God to idols of their own making.

Nor was he passing judgment on his own generation only; he was al-luding to mankind as a whole. Thus in the Sermon on the Mount he said: "If you then, who are evil, know how to give good gifts to your children, how much more will your Father who is in heaven give good things to those who ask him!" (Matt. 7:11) This statement is particularly striking because it concedes that fallen men can give "good" gifts; ... and at the same time they do not escape the designation "evil". That is, even when we see people at their very best, following the noble instincts of parenthood, Jesus still calls them "evil".

Jesus confirmed his view of man's sin and corruption by all his teaching about man's lostness and sickness (Luke 15; Matt. 9:12). His vivid meta-phors of the shepherd seeking the lost sheep and the physician healing the sick tell us as much about man's hopeless state as about his preciousness to the God who loves him.

Jesus taught that within the soil of every man's heart there lie buried the ugly seeds of every conceivable sin – "evil thoughts, acts of fornication, of theft, murder, adultery, ruthless greed and malice; fraud, indecency, envy, slander, arrogance, and folly. All thirteen are "evil things", and they come out of the heart of "the man" or "the men", every man. This is Jesus Christ's estimate of fallen human nature. ...

So then, according to Jesus, the "evil things" which we think, say and do are not due primarily to our environment, nor are they bad habits picked up from bad teaching, bad company or bad example; they are due to the inward corruption of our heart. This is not to say that environment, education and example are unimportant, for their influence for good or bad is very strong, and Christians should set themselves in these spheres to promote the good and eliminate the bad. What we are saying (because Jesus said it long ago) is that the dominant force in a person's life is his heredity, and that the ultimate origin of his evil thoughts and deeds is his evil heart, his nature which is twisted with self-centeredness. As God has said through the prophet Jeremiah centuries previously: "The heart is deceitful above all things, and desperately corrupt; who can understand it?" (Jer. 17:9). ... We say and do evil things because we have an evil heart or nature; it is from inside, out of our heart, that evil things and evil thoughts arise.

Modern psycho-analysis has tended only to confirm this teaching of the Old Testament which Jesus endorsed, because it has further uncovered the horrid secrets of the human heart. Psychology and experience tell us that the subconscious mind (which is roughly equivalent to what the Bible means by "heart", namely the center of our personality, the source of our thoughts and emotions) is like a deep well with a thick deposit of mud at the bottom. Normally, being at the bottom, the mud is safely out of sight. But when the well-waters are stirred, especially by the winds of violent emotion, the most evil-looking and evil-smelling filth breaks the surface – rage, spite, greed, lust, jealousy, malice, cruelty and revenge. These base passions keep bubbling up, raw and sinister, from the secret springs of the heart. And if we have any moral sensitivity, we must at times be appalled, shocked and disgusted by the foul things which lurk in the hidden depths of our personality.[34]

This understanding of human nature according to Jesus is as old as creation. Stott's belief in the historical view of the creation and fall of Adam and Eve flies in the face of a more generalized view of human origins. He believed that Scripture does not allow a mythical view of the first three chapters of Genesis despite acknowledging that there are some figurative elements in the narrative. He did not want to dogmatize about the seven days, the serpent, the tree of life, and the tree of the knowledge of good and evil. However he insisted that Adam and Eve were real people who were created good (innocent or ignorant of evil?) but were disobedient.[35] Stott held that, while evolution may have occurred over a long period of time, he was convinced it did not account for the creation of men and women, for the gap between humans and hominids was too wide. While our anatomy and physiology is linked to the animal world, there is a radical discontinuity of our uniqueness as the image of God.[36]

Stott backed up this interpretation by reference to the theological analogy of Adam and Christ in Romans 5:12–19 and 1 Corinthians 15:21,22,45–49. Paul depends on its validity, and on the historicity of both men. "Each is presented as the head of a race – fallen humanity owing to its ruin in Adam, and redeemed humanity owing its salvation to Christ. Death and condemnation are traced to Adam's disobedience, life and justification to Christ's obedience. The whole argument is built on two historical acts – the self-willed disobedience of Adam and the self-sacrificing obedience of Christ."[37]

Stott held that nothing in modern science contradicts this. Rather the reverse. This homogeneity of the human species is best explained by positing our descent from a common ancestor. Human fossil records were likely to have been pre-Adamic hominids. Adam, then, was a special creation of God, whether formed literally from the dust of the ground or out of an already existing hominid. "The vital truth we cannot surrender is that, though our bodies are related to the primates, we ourselves in our fundamental identity are related to God." How did Adam's special creation and subsequent fall relate to the other pre-Adamic hominids? He refers to Derek Kidner, who suggested that God conferred his image on Adam's collaterals, to bring them into the same realm of being. Adam's "federal" headship of humanity extended, if that was the case, outwards to his contemporaries as well as onwards to his offspring, and his disobedience disinherited both alike. Why did Adam die? "Death entered the world through sin" (Rom. 5:12). Scripture regards human death as unnatural – an alien intrusion, the penalty for sin – and not God's original intention for his human creation. It was not just spiritual death or separation from God. Physical death was included in the curse, and Adam became mortal when he disobeyed. It appears God had something better in mind for Adam and his successors, something less degrading and squalid than death, decay and decomposition, something that acknowledged that human beings are not animals.[38]

The Bible calls the disobedience of Adam "sin." Stott defined the nature of sin:

> But what is sin? Its universal extent is clear; what is its nature? Several words are used in the Bible to describe it. They group themselves into two categories, according to whether wrongdoing is regarded negatively or positively. Negatively, it is shortcoming. One word represents it as a lapse, a slip, a blunder. Another pictures it as the failure to hit a mark, as when throwing a spear at a target. Yet another shows it to be an inward badness, a disposition which falls short of what is good. Positively, sin is transgression. One word makes sin the trespass of a boundary. Another reveals it as lawlessness. Yet another as an act which violates justice. Both these groups of words imply the existence of a moral standard. It is either an ideal which we fail to reach, or a law which we break. "Whoever knows what is right to do and fails to do it, for him it is sin" (Jas. 4:17). That is the negative aspect. "Every one who commits sin is guilty of lawlessness" (1 John 3:4). That is the positive aspect.
>
> The Bible accepts the fact that men have different standards. The Jews have the law of Moses. The Gentiles have the law of conscience. But all

men have fallen short of their standard. All men have broken their law. It is the same for us. ... We all stand self-condemned. To some good-living people this comes as a genuine surprise. They have their ideals and think they attain them more or less. They do not indulge in much introspection. They are not unduly self-critical. They know they have occasional lapses. They are aware of certain character deficiencies. But they are not particularly alarmed by them and consider themselves no worse than the rest of men. All this is understandable enough, until we remember two things. Firstly, our sense of failure depends on how high our standards are. It is quite easy to consider oneself good at high jumping if the bar is never raised above 3ft. 6in. Secondly, God concerns himself with the thought behind the deed and with the motive behind the action. Jesus clearly taught this in the sermon on the mount, and we shall need to take it into consideration.[39]

He expounded at length three consequences of sin; which I summarize below:[40]

1. *Alienation from God.* Perhaps the most dreadful of all sin's consequences is that it estranges us from God. Man's highest destiny is to know God and to be in personal relationship with God. Man's chief claim to nobility is that he was made in the image of God and is therefore capable of knowing him. But this God whom we are meant to know and whom we ought to know is a moral Being. He is infinite in all his moral perfections. He is a holy God. He is a pure and righteous God. ... Our sins blot out God's face from us as effectively as the clouds do the sun. ... Until our sins are cleansed away, we are exiles. Our soul is lost. We have no communion with God. It is this which accounts for the restlessness of men and women today. There is a hunger in people's hearts that nothing can satisfy but God himself. There is a vacuum in man's soul that only God can fill. ... The situation is tragic beyond words. People are missing the destiny for which God made them.

2. *Bondage to Self,* the inwardness of sin, which Stott describes as a deep-seated inward corruption. It is what theologians mean by "original sin."[41]

   It is a tendency or bias towards sin and self-centeredness, which we inherit, which is rooted deeply in our human personality and, which manifests itself in a thousand ugly ways. ... It is because sin is an inward corruption of human nature that we are in bondage. It is not so much certain acts or habits that enslave us but the evil infection from which these spring. ... We have high ideals but weak wills. We want to live a good life but we are chained and imprisoned. We are not free. We are slaves.[42]

3. **Conflict with Others**. William Temple's definition of original sin perfectly describes this truth: "I am the center of the world I see; where the horizon is depends on where I stand. ... Education may make my self-centeredness less disastrous by widening my horizon of interest; so far it is like climbing a tower that widens the horizon for physical vision while leaving me still the center and standard of reference."[43]

Stott concludes that Christianity is a "rescue religion." People do not appreciate it unless they know they need to be rescued.

In his commentary on Romans 3:9–20, he identifies seven Old Testament quotations Paul draws on to describe "sin." Three features of the grim biblical picture they paint, stand out.[44]

First, it declares *the ungodliness of sin*. Scripture identifies the essence of sin as ungodliness (cf. 1:18). Sin is the revolt of the self against God, the dethronement of God with a view to the enthronement of oneself. Ultimately sin is self-deification, the reckless determination to occupy the throne that belongs to God alone.

Secondly, this range of Old Testament verses teaches *the pervasiveness of sin*. For sin affects every part of our human constitution, every faculty and function, including our mind, emotions, sexuality, conscience and will. This is the biblical doctrine of "total depravity," which Stott suspects is repudiated only by those who misunderstand it. It has never meant that human beings are as depraved as they could possibly be. Such a notion is manifestly absurd and untrue and is contradicted by our everyday observation. Not all human beings are drunkards, felons, adulterers or murderers. No, the "totality" of our corruption refers to its extent (twisting and tainting every part of our humanness) not to its degree (depraving every part of us absolutely).

Unredeemed sinners can love. Parental love, filial love, conjugal love, the love of friends – all these, as we know very well, are the regular experience of men and women outside Christ. Even the tax collectors love those who love them. Even the Gentiles salute each other. None of this is in dispute. But all human love, even the highest, the noblest and the best, is contaminated to some degree by the impurities of self-interest. We Christians are specifically called to love our enemies (in which love there is no self-interest), and this is impossible without the supernatural grace of God.[45]

Thirdly, the Old Testament quotations teach *the universality of sin*, both negatively and positively. Every mouth is stopped, every excuse silenced, and the whole world, having been found guilty, is liable to God's judgment.

Therefore, no-one will be declared righteous in his sight by observing the law (Rom. 3:20).

In conclusion, how should we respond to Paul's devastating exposure of universal sin and guilt, as we read it today? We should not try to evade it by changing the subject and talking instead of the need for self-esteem, or by blaming our behavior on our genes, nurturing, education or society. It is an essential part of our dignity as human beings that, however much we may have been affected by negative influences, we are not their helpless victims, but rather responsible for our conduct. We have no merit to plead and no excuse to make. We too stand before God speechless and condemned.[46]

The influence of Charles Simeon was so strong in Stott that, in his Introduction to a series of Simeon's sermons, he highlighted the principal mark of regeneration as an awareness of one's sinfulness:

At one of his weekly tea-parties somebody asked Simeon: "What, Sir, do you consider the principal mark of regeneration?" It was a probing question. ... This was Simeon's answer: "the very first and indispensable thing is self-loathing and abhorrence. Nothing short of this can be admitted as an evidence of a real change. ... I want to see more of this humble, contrite, broken spirit amongst us. It is the very spirit that belongs to self-condemned sinners. ... This sitting in the dust is most pleasing to God ... give me to be with a broken-hearted Christian, and I prefer his society to that of all the rest. ... Were I now to addressing to you my dying words, I should say nothing else but what I have just said. Try to live in this spirit of self-abhorrence, and let it habitually mark your life and conduct" (Carus, pp.651–52).

"Self-loathing", "self-condemnation", "self-abhorrence". The words grate on modern ears. The contemporary craze is for a bigger and better self-image. We are exhorted on all sides to love ourselves, forgive ourselves, respect ourselves, assert ourselves. And to be sure, as in all heresies, there are a few grains of truth in this one. For we should gratefully affirm ourselves as children of God redeemed by Christ and indwelt by his Spirit. In this mercy of God our Creator and Savior we are to rejoice greatly, and there is much exhortation to such joy in Simeon's sermons.

But to rejoice in God is one thing; to rejoice in ourselves is another. Self-congratulation and the worship of God are mutually incompatible. Those who have a high view of themselves always have a corresponding low view of God. It is those who have seen God high and lifted up, exalted in indescribable glory above the universe, who become overwhelmed with a sense of their own sinfulness and unworthiness. ... Modern men and women may value "self-esteem", but God thinks differently. "This is the one I esteem," he says: "he who is humble and contrite in spirit, and trembles at my word" (Is. 66:2).

Our proud, self-confident, self-congratulatory generation urgently needs to recover this biblical perspective. I do myself. It is the acme of health and holiness.[47]

I can testify to Stott expressing this when in prayer meetings he would begin by echoing the words of Abraham, "Now that I have been bold as to speak to the Lord, though I am nothing but dust and ashes" (Gen. 18:27). This low view of humanity in sin is characterized by the wages of sin, which is death (Rom. 6:23). In his commentary on Ephesians, when he expounds Paul's description of humanity as being "dead in transgressions and sins" (Eph. 2:1,5), he interprets the phrase as meaning "deadness of soul," which is experienced by non-Christian people. While they may be alive in their bodies, minds, and personalities, they have no life in their souls.

> They are blind to the glory of Jesus Christ, and deaf to the voice of the Holy Spirit. They have no love for God, no sensitive awareness of his personal reality, no leaping of their spirit toward him in the cry, "*Abba*, Father", no longing for fellowship with his people. They are as unresponsive to him as a corpse. So we should not hesitate to affirm that a life without God (however physically fit and mentally alert the person may be) is a living death, and that those who live it are dead even while they are living (1 Tim. 5:6). To affirm this paradox is to become aware of the basic tragedy of fallen human existence. It is that people who were created by God and for God should now be living without God. Indeed, that was our condition until the Good Shepherd found us.[48]

Stott contrasts what we are by nature and what we are by grace. The human condition is rectified by divine compassion. "Christians are sometimes criticized for being morbidly preoccupied with their sin and guilt. The criticism is not fair when we are facing the facts about ourselves (for it is never unhealthy to look reality in the face), but only when we fail to go on to glory in God's mercy and grace."[49]

5

The Cross

John Stott's ashes were buried in the graveyard of St. James the Great Church in Dale, Pembrokeshire, Wales. He had asked that a gravestone would be placed there with the words borrowed from Charles Simeon's memorial in Holy Trinity, Cambridge. After Stott's name and dates, 1921–2011, are the words,

WHO RESOLVED
BOTH AS THE GROUND OF HIS SALVATION
AND AS THE SUBJECT OF HIS MINISTRY
TO KNOW NOTHING EXCEPT
JESUS CHRIST
AND HIM CRUCIFIED
1 CORINTHIANS 2:2

'The Cross of Christ' and many other books were written at his retreat, The Hookses, Dale

The Cross of Christ, published by InterVarsity Press in 1986, is considered to be Stott's magnum opus. He began by establishing the centrality of the cross in the mind of Christ, in Scripture, and in history. In answer to the question "Why did Christ die?" he maintained both that the Father "gave him up" and that Jesus "gave himself up" for us. He broached the problem of forgiveness, as constituted by the conflict between the majesty of God and the gravity of sin, and concluded that God must "satisfy himself." That is, he cannot contradict himself, but must act in a way that expresses his perfect character of holy love. He did this by substituting himself in Christ for us. Stott then affirmed "self-satisfaction by self-substitution" as the essence of the cross.

He wrote that the cross enforced three truths – about ourselves, about God, and about Jesus Christ.

> First, our sin must be extremely horrible. Nothing reveals the gravity of sin like the cross. For ultimately what sent Christ there was neither the greed of Judas, nor the envy of the priests, nor the vacillating cowardice of Pilate, but our own greed, envy, cowardice and other sins, and Christ's resolve in love and mercy to bear their judgment and so put them away. It is impossible for

us to face Christ's cross with integrity and not to feel ashamed of ourselves. Apathy, selfishness and complacency blossom everywhere in the world except at the cross. There these noxious reeds shrivel and die. They are seen for the tatty, poisonous things they are. For if there was no way by which the righteous God could righteously forgive our unrighteousness, except that he should bear it himself in Christ, it must be serious indeed. It is only when we see this that, stripped of our self-righteousness and self-satisfaction, we are ready to put our trust in Jesus Christ as the Savior we urgently need.

Secondly, God's love must be wonderful beyond comprehension. God could quite justly have abandoned us to our fate. He could have left us alone to reap the fruit of our wrongdoing and to perish in our sins. It is what we deserved. But he did not. Because he loved us, he came after us in Christ. He pursued us even to the desolate anguish of the cross, where he bore our sin, guilt, judgment and death. It takes a hard and stony heart to remain unmoved by love like that. It is more than love. Its proper name is "grace", which is love to the undeserving.

Thirdly, Christ's salvation must be a free gift. He "purchased" it for us at the high price of his own life-blood. So what is there left for us to pay? Nothing! Since he claimed that all was now "finished". There is nothing for us to contribute. Not of course that we now have a license to sin and can always count on God's forgiveness. On the contrary, the same cross of Christ, which is the ground of a free salvation, is also the most powerful incentive to a holy life. But this new life follows. First, we have to humble ourselves at the foot of the cross, confess that we have sinned and deserve nothing at his hand but judgment, thank him that he loved us and died for us, and receive from him full and free forgiveness. Against this self-humbling our ingrained pride rebels. We resent the idea that we cannot earn – or even contribute to – our own salvation. So we stumble, as Paul put it, over the stumbling block of the cross.[50]

The essence of the cross being "self-satisfaction by self-substitution" cannot be understood without appreciating, and taking seriously, the nature of God as holy love. Forgiveness of sins required satisfaction. The sacrificial system of the tabernacle and temple worship in the Old Testament witnessed to the gravity of sin and the costly nature of forgiveness. At the very heart of the church's worship is this realization.

Thomas Cranmer included a clear statement of it at the beginning of his Prayer of Consecration in the Book of Common Prayer (1549). In consequence, for 400 years Anglicans have described Jesus Christ as having made on the cross, by his "one oblation of himself once offered", "a full, perfect, and sufficient sacrifice, oblation, and satisfaction for the sins of the whole world."

But the way in which different theologians have developed the concept of satisfaction depends on their understanding of the obstacles to forgiveness which need first to be removed. What demands are being made which stand in the way until they are satisfied? And who is making them? Is it the devil? Or is it the law, or God's honor or justice, or "the moral order"? All these have been proposed, I shall argue, however that the primary "obstacle" is to be found within God himself. He must "satisfy himself" in the way of salvation he devises; he cannot save us by contradicting himself.[51]

Stott turns to Emil Brunner, who in his famous book *The Mediator* gave a most helpful elucidation of the inviolability of the moral order of the universe. Sin is more than "an attack on God's honor," Brunner wrote; it is an assault on the moral world order, which is an expression of God's moral will.

The law of his divine Being, on which all the law and order in the world is based. ... the logical and reliable character of all that happens, the validity of all standards, of all intellectual, legal and moral order, the Law itself, in its most profound meaning, demands the divine reaction, the divine concern about sin, the divine resistance to this rebellion and this breach of order. ... If this were not true, then there would be no seriousness in the world at all; there would be no meaning in anything, no order, no stability; the world order would fall into ruins, chaos and desolation would be supreme. All order in the world depends on the inviolability of his (sc. God's) honor, upon the certitude that those who rebel against him will be punished.[52]

Sin has caused "a break in the world order," a disorder so deep-seated that reparation or restitution is necessary, that is, "Atonement."[53] Two complementary truths about God are brought together: God as Holy and Righteous, and God as Loving and Merciful; to remind us we must beware of speaking of one aspect of God's character without remembering its counterpart. Brunner in *The Mediator* did not hesitate to write of God's "dual nature" as "the central mystery of the Christian revelation."[54] For "God is not simply Love. The nature of God cannot be exhaustively stated in one single word."[55] Indeed, modern opposition to forensic language in relation to the cross is mainly "due to the fact that the idea of the Divine Holiness has been swallowed up in that of the Divine Love; this means that the biblical idea of God, in which the decisive element is this twofold nature of holiness and love, is being replaced by the modern, unilateral, monistic idea of God."[56] Yet, "the dualism of holiness and love ... or mercy and wrath cannot be dissolved, changed into one synthetic conception, without at the same time destroying the seriousness of the biblical knowledge of God, the reality and the mystery of revelation and atonement. ... So then, the cross of Christ is the event in which God makes known his holiness and his love simultaneously, in one event, in an absolute manner."[57] … "The cross is the only place where the loving, forgiving, merciful God is revealed in such a way that we perceive that his holiness and his love are equally infinite."[58]

In fact, Brunner concludes "the objective aspect of the atonement … may be summed up thus: it consists in the combination of inflexible righteousness, with its penalties, and transcendent love,"[59] and Stott summarizes:

> This vision of God's holy love will deliver us from caricatures of him. We must picture him neither as an indulgent God who compromises his holiness in order to spare and spoil us, nor as a harsh and vindictive God who suppresses his love in order to crush and destroy us. How then can God express his holiness without consuming us, and his love without condoning our sins? How can God satisfy his holy love? How can he save us and satisfy himself simultaneously? We reply at this point only that, in order to satisfy himself, he sacrificed – indeed substituted – himself for us.[60]

In Chapter 6 of *The Cross of Christ*, entitled "The Self-Substitution of God," Stott explored all the different interpretations of this subject. He reviewed the nature of sacrifice in the Old Testament, the Passover and the history of various theologies dealing with "sin-bearing." Christ bore the penalty of our sin instead of us. He took our curse, so that we may receive his blessing; he became sin with our sin, so that we may become righteous with his righteousness (Rom. 4:6; 1 Cor. 1:30; Phil. 3:9). The cross was a substitutionary sacrifice. Christ died instead of us.

The question then becomes: who exactly is our substitute? Who took our place and bore our sin? How are we to think of him? This is where some preachers get it wrong when they use illustrations to drive home their point. I have heard preachers use the story of a father having to choose between saving his son and saving passengers on a train. Then there are those who would portray a compassionate Christ inducing a reluctant God to take action on our behalf. "We must not think of God punishing Jesus or of Jesus persuading God, for to do so is to set them over against each other as if they acted independently of each other or were even in conflict with each other."[61] Nor is it correct to say that the Father is the sacrifice, for the Father sent the Son. We must not confuse the persons of the Trinity.

> Our substitute, then, who took our place and died our death on the cross, was neither Christ alone (since that would make him a third party thrust in between God and us), nor God alone (since that would undermine the historical incarnation) but God in Christ, who was truly and fully God and man, and who on that account was uniquely qualified to represent both God and man and to mediate between them. If we speak only of Christ

suffering and dying, we overlook the initiative of the Father. If we speak only of God suffering and dying, we overlook the mediation of the Son. The New Testament authors never attribute the atonement either to Christ in such a way as to disassociate him from the Father, or to God in such a way as to dispense with Christ, but rather to God and Christ, or to God acting in and through Christ with his whole-hearted concurrence.[62] ...

The biblical gospel of atonement is of God satisfying himself by substituting himself for us. ... The concept of substitution may be said, then, to lie at the heart of both sin and salvation. For the essence of sin is man substituting himself for God, while the essence of salvation is God substituting himself for man.[63]

Stott looked beyond the cross itself to its consequences – its achievement – in three spheres: (1) the salvation of sinners, (2) the revelation of God, and (3) the conquest of evil.

1. As for **salvation** he studied the four words "redemption," "propitiation," "justification," and "reconciliation." These are New Testament "images," metaphors of what God has done in and through Christ's death.

> *"Redemption"* is a commercial term borrowed from the marketplace. We were slaves or captives in bondage to our sin and guilt, and utterly unable to liberate ourselves. But Jesus Christ "redeemed" us, bought us out of captivity, shedding his blood as the ransom price.

> To *"propitiate"* somebody means to placate his or her anger. This seems to many to be an unworthy concept of God. Paul is describing God's solution to the human predicament, which is not only sin but God's wrath upon sin (Rom. 1:18; 2:5; 3:5). We should not shy of using the word "propitiation" in relation to the cross any more than we should drop the word "wrath" in relation to God. First, why is a propitiation necessary? God's holy wrath rests on evil. Secondly, who undertakes to do the propitiating? God in his undeserved love has done for us what we could never do by ourselves. Thirdly, how has the propitiation been accomplished? God gave his own Son to die in our place, and in giving his Son he gave himself (5:8; 8:32). The cross vindicated the justice of God. The contrast is between the sins committed beforehand or previously and in the present time; between the divine forbearance that postponed judgment and the divine justice that exacted it; between the leaving unpunished former sins and their punishment on the cross. God left unpunished the sins of former generations not because of any injustice on his part or with any thought of condoning evil, but in his forbearance, and only because it was his fixed intention in the fulness

of time to punish those sins in the death of his Son. This was the only way in which he could be both just and the one who justifies those who have faith in Jesus.

"Justification" is a legal or forensic term belonging to the law courts. Its opposite is "condemnation." Both are the pronouncements of a judge. Justification is not just forgiveness. Pardon is negative, the remission of a penalty or debt; justification is positive, the bestowal of a righteous status, the sinner's reinstatement in favor and fellowship with God. Justification does not mean sanctification or "making just" as is the Roman Catholic view. The means of our justification is faith. Justification is by grace alone, in Christ alone, through faith alone. The value of faith is not to be found in itself, but entirely and exclusively in its object, namely Jesus Christ and him crucified. Faith is the eye that looks to him, the hand that receives his free gift, the mouth that drinks the living water. Justification is the heart of the gospel and unique to Christianity. All other systems teach some sort of self-salvation through good works of religion, righteousness or philanthropy. Emil Brunner illustrated it vividly in terms of the difference between "ascent" and "descent." The really "decisive question," he wrote, is "the direction of the movement." Non-Christian systems think of "the self-movement of man" toward God. None of these has seen or felt the gulf that yawns between the holy God and sinful, guilty human beings. Only when we glimpse this do we grasp the necessity of what the gospel proclaims, namely "the self-movement of God," his free initiative of grace, his "descent," his amazing "act of condescension."[64]

"Reconciliation" is the fourth image of salvation in which our relationship with God and one another is made one. This is the meaning of atonement.

Substitution is not another image of salvation; it is the reality that lies behind all four images.

2. Stott next explains that God has fully and finally **revealed** his love and justice by exercising them in the cross. When substitution is denied, God's self-disclosure is obscured; but when it is affirmed, his glory shines forth brightly.

3. Having concentrated on the cross as both objective achievement (salvation from sin) and subjective influence (through the revelation of holy love), Stott explored the theme *Christus Victor* as a third biblical consequence

of the cross. It depicts **Christ's victory** over the devil, the law, the flesh, the world, and death; and our victory through him.

The final section in *The Cross of Christ* was entitled "Living Under the Cross," because the Christian community is essentially a community of the cross. The cross has radically altered all our relationships. We now worship God in continuous celebration, understand ourselves and give ourselves in the service of others, love our enemies by seeking to overcome evil with good, and face the perplexing problem of suffering in the light of the cross.[65]

In the last chapter Stott sought to answer the questions: What is the relationship between Christ's sufferings and ours? How does the cross speak to us in our pain? He gave six possible answers:

First, the cross of Christ is **a stimulus to patient endurance**. Undeserved suffering is part of our Christian calling and Jesus left us an example to inspire us to persevere (1 Pet. 2:18–23).

Secondly, the cross of Christ is **the path to mature holiness**. Jesus learned obedience from what he suffered (Heb. 5:8–9) and was made perfect (Heb. 2:10). Through suffering we are disciplined, refined and pruned. God intends suffering to be a means of grace.

Thirdly, the cross of Christ is **the symbol of suffering service** (John 12:23–26, 32–33).

The place of suffering in service and of passion in mission is hardly ever taught today. But the greatest single secret of evangelism or missionary effectiveness is the willingness to suffer and die. It may be a death to popularity (by faithfully preaching the unpopular biblical gospel), or to pride (by the use of modest methods in reliance on the Holy Spirit), or to racial and national prejudice (by identification with another culture), or to material comfort (by adopting a simple lifestyle). But the servant must suffer if he is to bring light to the nations, and the seed must die if it is to multiply.[66]

Fourthly, the cross of Christ is **the hope of final glory**. The hope of glory makes suffering bearable (Rom. 8:18,28–29). However, Scripture gives us no liberty to assert that all human suffering leads to glory.

Fifthly, the cross of Christ is **the ground of a reasonable faith**. "If it was reasonable for Job to trust the God whose wisdom and power have been revealed in creation, how much more reasonable is it for us to trust the God whose love and justice have been revealed in the cross?"[67]

Sixthly, the cross of Christ **is the proof of God's solidary love**, that is, of his personal, loving solidarity with us in our pain. We are not to envisage God indifferent to us but on a cross suffering with us. "There is good biblical evidence that God not only suffered in Christ, but that God in Christ suffers with his people still. ... I could never myself believe in God, if it were not for the cross. ... In the real world of pain, how could one worship a God who was immune to it?. ... He laid aside his immunity to pain. He entered our world of flesh and blood, tears and death. He suffered for us."[68]

6

Holy Scripture

I attended the Evangelical Fellowship in the Anglican Communion's consultation at the University of Kent at Canterbury, England in June 1993. John Stott gave five expositions of Scripture under the title of "The Anglican Communion and Scripture": (1) *The God of Revelation* (Isa. 55); (2) *Light in the Darkness* (2 Pet. 1:12–21); (3) *The Spirit of Truth* (John 14–16); (4) *The Holy Spirit and the Holy Bible* (1 Cor. 2:6–16); and (5) *Continuing in the Word* (2 Tim. 3:14–17). He concluded his second exposition by saying: "Because Scripture is the word of God, we read it like no other book, humbly, on our knees, crying to the Holy Spirit for illumination. Because Scripture is also the word of men, we read it like every other book, paying attention to its historical and geographical background, its cultural context, its literary genre, its grammar, syntax and vocabulary. We study it diligently."

It is this humble and balanced perspective that characterized Stott's view of the Scriptures. In this he followed his mentor, Charles Simeon, who wrote:

> I soon learned that I must take the Scriptures with the simplicity of a little child, and be content to receive on God's testimony, what he has revealed, whether I can unravel all the difficulties that attend it or not; and from that day to this I have never had a doubt respecting the truth of that doctrine, nor a wish (as far as I know) to be wise above what is written. I feel that I cannot even explain how it is that I move my finger, and therefore I am content to be ignorant of innumerable things which exceed, not only my wisdom, but the most learned men in the universe. For this disposition of mind I have unbounded reason to be thankful to God; for I have not only avoided many perplexities by means of it, but actually learned much, which I should otherwise have never learned. I was not then aware that this simple exercise of faith is the only way of attaining divine knowledge; but I now see it is so; and in fact, it is the true way in which we attain human knowledge also; for the child receives everything first upon the authority of his teacher, and thus learns the very first rudiments of language. ... he calls things as he is taught to call them, and then, in due time, he sees that

these things are not the arbitrary dictates of his master, but that they of necessity appertain to language, and exist in the very nature of things; and thus in time he comes to see a beauty and propriety in things which were at first no better to him than senseless jargon. This, I am persuaded, is the way in which we should receive instruction from God; and if we will do so, I verily believe, that we shall in due time see a beauty and harmony in many things, which the pertinacious advocates of human systems can never understand.[69]

In preparation for the National Evangelical Anglican Congress in April 1967 Stott contributed an essay to *Guidelines*, edited by J.I. Packer, entitled "Jesus Christ our Teacher and Lord – towards solving the problem of authority." He addressed the doctrinal confusion in contemporary Christendom as stemming from a lack of agreement on the question of authority. He wrote:

> The evangelical position has always been the same, namely that we are under the authority of Christ; that in these last days God has spoken to us in his Son; that this Divine Son, the Word made flesh, Jesus Christ of Nazareth, is as much the Mediator of a final revelation as of a finished redemption, that, according to Christ, this revelation is coterminous with Scripture; that submission to the authority of Christ must therefore involve submission to the authority of Scripture; and that, although human reason and Church tradition play an important part in the elucidation of Scripture, their part must always be subordinate to the Scripture itself as being the Word, not of men, but of God.[70]

He explored the knowledge and authority of Jesus Christ and argued that he was the Word made flesh, the divine-human Person who can be trusted as our Teacher. But can we trust that the Gospels accurately report what he said and did? They are eye-witness accounts that were written down, but many doubt their authenticity.

> The most radical Form Critics have treated the historical contexts in which the various Gospel incidents or teachings are set as entirely unreliable, having been supplied by the church or teacher using them, and have even argued that much of the material itself was freely invented by the Christian community in the interests of evangelism, apologetic, or catechism. This view has been forcibly challenged by a number of writers, and particularly by Norwegian scholars from the University of Uppsala: Harald Riesenfeld and Birger Gerhardsson. As a Rabbi Jesus would have trained his apostles by constant repetition and perhaps by singing, to learn his teaching by heart until they had it word perfect. Phenomenal feats of Jewish memory are claimed (including the memorization of the whole Old Testament,

together with the chief commentaries on it), and why should not similar feats have been performed by the apostles.[71]

Christians accept the authority of the Old Testament because Christ did. He regarded it as the word of God and quoted it freely. He commissioned and inspired the apostles to teach what the Holy Spirit would bring to their remembrance in his name. Their teaching comprises the New Testament. We maintain the perspicuity of Scripture, that is, that the essential teaching of Scripture is plain and self-evident. Stott's conclusion is "that submission to Scripture, and Scripture only, is the only Christian solution to the problem of authority, because it is included in and required by our submission to Christ."[72]

In *The Message of Galatians*, Stott addressed two alternative interpretations to the authority of Scripture.

> The first was the view of **radical theologians** who questioned the authority of the apostles by their own wisdom, e.g. C.H. Dodd who wrote,
>
> > "Sometimes I think Paul is wrong, and I have ventured to say so." But we have no liberty to think or venture thus. The apostles of Jesus Christ were unique – unique in their experience of the Jesus of history, unique in their sight of the risen Lord, unique in their commission by Christ's authority and unique in their inspiration by Christ's Spirit. We may not exalt our opinions over theirs or claim that our authority is as great as theirs. For their opinions and authority are Christ's. If we would bow to His authority, we must therefore bow to theirs.[73]
>
> The second questioning of the authority of Scripture comes from **the Roman Catholic Church**, who used to teach that the church wrote the Bible and that, therefore, "the Church is over the Bible and has authority not only to interpret it, but also to supplement it." Stott argued that the apostles were apostles of Christ, not of the church, so that the apostles derived their authority from God through Christ. "Apostolic authority is divine authority. It is neither human nor ecclesiastical. And because it is divine we must submit to it."[74]

Stott took issue with those who viewed the Scriptures as historical documents that are limited by their cultural origins and therefore dated as to their applicability today.

> This is an extremely serious charge. If true, it would mean that we can reject whole portions of Scripture on the ground that "that is what they thought in those days, but we know better." This attitude I cannot accept. It seems to me clearly in conflict with the inspiration of Scripture, that is, the process by which God himself spoke through the human authors. It

also overlooks the fact that God's people were called to be different from others, not to conform to this world, but to challenge their own culture in the name of Christ. [*Essentials: a liberal-evangelical dialogue.* Copyright ©1988 David L. Edwards & John R.W. Stott. Reproduced by permission of Hodder and Stoughton Limited][75]

He recognized the problem of our own cultural imprisonment and the problem of the cultural conditioning of the biblical authors: "there is a collision of cultures between the biblical world and the modern world."[76] The hermeneutical challenge is that we must be careful not to interpret the Scriptures according to our own cultural perspective. Careful exegesis of the text necessitates studying it in its own cultural terms. How can a divine revelation given in transient cultural terms have permanent validity? How can a revelation addressed to a particular cultural situation have a universal application? He commended cultural transposition: "identify the essential revelation in the text (what God is saying here), to separate this from the cultural form in which he chose to give it, and then to re-clothe it in appropriate modern cultural terms."[77]

> Cultural transposition cannot be used to justify the rejection of what Scripture teaches, forbids or commands. The reason for the biblical prohibitions of homosexual conduct was not cultural, but creational. They arose from the biblical definition of marriage, which was personally endorsed by Jesus Christ (Gen. 2:24; Mark 10:7–9). What limits sexual intercourse to heterosexual marriage, and forbids it in other relationships, is not culture but creation. Cultural transposition is not a conveniently respectable way to dodge awkward passages of Scripture by declaring them to be culturally relative. It is not a sophisticated way of rejecting biblical authority.[78]

Stott taught three principles of interpretation: simplicity, history, and harmony.

First is *the natural meaning* of Scripture, because God intended his revelation to be a plain and readily intelligible communication to ordinary human beings. According to its literary genre it may be interpreted literally or figuratively.

Secondly comes *the original meaning*, because God addressed his word to those who first heard it, and it can be received by subsequent generations only in so far as they understand it historically. The text must be understood in terms of its context.

Thirdly is *the general meaning*, because God cannot contradict himself and is self-consistent. Scripture is without error in all that it affirms.

As chief architect of the Lausanne Covenant and its exposition, Stott affirmed its second section on the authority and power of the Bible.

> We affirm the divine inspiration, truthfulness and authority of both Old and New Testament Scriptures in their entirety as the written word of God, without error in all that it affirms, and the only infallible rule of faith and practice. We also affirm the power of God's word to accomplish his purpose of salvation. The message of the Bible is addressed to all men and women. For God's revelation in Christ and in Scripture is unchangeable. Through it the Holy Spirit still speaks today. He illumines the minds of God's people in every culture to perceive its truth freshly through their own eyes and thus discloses to the whole church ever more of the many-colored wisdom of God.[79]

7

Salvation

When I was studying for my theological degree at Durham University my Principal at Cranmer Hall, St. John's College, was Jim Hickinbotham. When he became Principal of Wycliffe Hall, Oxford he invited John Stott to deliver a series of public lectures known as the Chavasse Lectures in World Mission. They were published in 1975 as *Christian Mission in the Modern World*. In the Foreword, Hickinbotham described Stott's lectures as biblical and clear. "He is an exact and rigorous thinker who cuts through ambiguities and obscurities, and compels us to face theological issues, logically and precisely."[80] Further, he said, Stott was fair. "He always qualifies his criticisms so as to avoid any injustice to those whom he criticizes and he balances criticism by generous recognition of the true and good things which those with whom he disagrees are saying and standing for."[81] Lastly, he wrote, Stott was constructive. "He speaks and writes with the courtesy and warm friendship which Christians owe to one another when they are discussing their differences."[82]

Stott devoted a whole chapter (lecture) to the topic of "Salvation" and compared the biblical understanding with modern reconstructions. He began with the meeting of the Commission on World Mission and Evangelism of the World Council of Churches in Bangkok in January 1973, entitled "Salvation Today." It prompted him to question whether the Bangkok interpretation of salvation was true to the teaching of Jesus and his apostles. Christianity is a religion of salvation – God has taken the initiative to save us – he is called our Savior – Jesus "came into the world to save sinners" (1 Tim. 1:15) – the name Jesus means "God the Savior" or "God is salvation" (Matt. 1:21) and his full title is "our Lord and Savior Jesus Christ" (2 Pet. 3:18) – the Bible is "able to instruct you for salvation through faith in Jesus Christ" (2 Tim. 3:15) – and the gospel is "the power of God for salvation" (Rom. 1:16). He then went on to differentiate the biblical understanding of salvation from the ecumenical movement's definition.

First, *salvation does not mean psycho-physical health*. It is not "wholeness" despite healings being signs of the kingdom of God that Jesus came to bring. Salvation may bring healing of mind and body but healing today is not salvation; for not until the resurrection and redemption of our bodies will disease and death be no more. Salvation is not a kind of psychological integration, the wholeness of a balanced personality. As the son of an eminent physician Stott believed that the role of the doctor and the pastor can become confused. A physician can replace the pastor, or the pastor can see himself as an amateur psychologist and counselor. He quoted Dr Martyn Lloyd-Jones, who gave up being a physician in order to become a celebrated preacher: "The Hospital does not, cannot, and never will be able to take over the functions of the Church! It is quite impossible for it to do so ... The authentic task of the Church is not primarily to make people healthy ... her essential task is to restore men to right relationship with God ... Man's real problem is not simply that he is sick, but that he is a rebel."[83]

While the word "save" is used in the New Testament for various kinds of deliverance from material harm it is not a comprehensive insurance against physical ills of every kind. Salvation is a rescue from sin. It is moral not material. Sin is a chronic inward moral disease. The healings and deliverances from danger were illustrations of salvation, not promises of safety or health.

Secondly, *salvation is not socio-political liberation*. The emphasis of the World Council of Churches was "the liberation from social and political structures of inequality and oppression. It reinterprets salvation as the liberation of deprived and disadvantaged people from hunger, poverty and war, from colonial domination, political tyranny, racial discrimination and economic exploitation, from the ghettos, the political prisons and the soulless technology of the modern world."[84] While these are desirable goals, pleasing to God the Creator for the God of the Bible is a God of justice and he hates injustice and tyranny, it is not what the Bible calls salvation.

Stott quoted at length from *A Theology of Liberation* by Gustavo Gutierrez. In a critical review he highlights the problems he has with the book while admiring the deep compassion of Gutierrez, who confused Marxist categories with Christian theology. "It is to mix what Scripture keeps distinct – God the Creator and God the Redeemer, the God of the cosmos and the God of the covenant, the world and the church, common grace and saving grace, justice and justification, the reformation of society and the regeneration of men. For the salvation offered in the gospel of Christ concerns persons rather than structures. It is deliverance from another kind of yoke than political and economic oppression."[85] He questioned the literal interpretation of biblical passages such as the Exodus and Christ's proclamation of the fulfillment of Isaiah 61:1,2 in

Nazareth (Luke 4:18). Deliverance from slavery, poverty, blindness, and unjust imprisonment should provoke our Christian concern but it is not the salvation Christ died and rose to secure for us.

Stott went on to define salvation as personal freedom: freedom from sin in all its ugly manifestations for a life of service. It is a process of justification, sanctification, and glorification: past, present, and future.

> Salvation is freedom. ... It includes freedom from the just judgment of God on our sins, from our guilt and our guilty conscience, into new relationship with him in which we become his reconciled, forgiven children and we know him as our Father. It is freedom from the bitter bondage of meaninglessness into a new sense of purpose in God's new society of love, in which the last are first, the poor rich and the meek heirs. It is freedom from the dark prison of our own self-centeredness into a new life of self-fulfillment through self-forgetful service. And one day it will include freedom from the futility of pain, decay, death and dissolution into a new world of immortality, beauty and unimaginable joy. All this – and more! – is "salvation."[86]

Later in 1975 he was invited to attend the World Council of Churches Assembly in Nairobi as an advisor. He used his time to urge the WCC to recover the biblical understanding of salvation. When he returned to his seat after his presentation, Dr Krister Stendahl, who was teaching at Harvard Divinity School, leaned over and commented, "I did not agree with one word you said!"[87] Such characterizes the divide between evangelical and liberal theologies.

What then *is* salvation?

It is deliverance from sin, the liberation of men and women from the consequences of sin. It is a comprehensive term covering our forgiveness and reconciliation to God. "It embraces not only our acceptance with God, but our progressive liberation from the tyranny of selfishness and the restoration of harmonious relations with our fellow men. The first of these is by the death of Christ, but it is by his Spirit that we can be set free from ourselves and by his church that we can be united in a fellowship of love."[88]

> Salvation is far more than forgiveness. We are called to be holy. The term "salvation" urgently needs to be rescued from the mean and meagre concepts to which we tend to degrade it. "Salvation" is a majestic word, denoting that comprehensive purpose of God by which he justifies, sanctifies, and glorifies his people: first pardoning our offenses and accepting us as righteous in his sight through Christ, then progressively transforming us by his Spirit into the image of his Son until, finally, we become like Christ in heaven, with new bodies in a new world. We must not minimize the greatness of "such a great salvation" (Heb. 2:3).[89]

Commenting on 2 Timothy 1:9,10 Stott traced the river of salvation to its source back beyond time in a past eternity. He addressed the doctrines of predestination and election, which emphasize that salvation is due to God's grace alone and not to human merit; not to our works performed in time but to God's purpose conceived in eternity. God first decided for us before we decided for him. Human beings are by nature blind, deaf, and dead. Our conversion is impossible unless God gives us sight, hearing, and life.

Predestination is said to foster arrogance but, on the contrary, *it excludes boasting*.

Predestination is said to foster uncertainty and to create in people a neurotic anxiety as to whether they are saved or not. But believers know that in the end their security lies only in the eternal, predestinating will of God. Nothing else can *bring such assurance and comfort*.

Predestination is said to foster apathy; that all human responsibility before God has been undermined. On the contrary, *God's sovereignty never diminishes our responsibility*. Instead, the two lie side by side in an antinomy – an apparent contradiction between two truths.

Predestination is said to foster complacency, for why should we not live as we please, without moral restraint? Paul answered this in *Romans 6*.

Predestination is said to foster narrow-mindedness; the elect people of God can become absorbed only in themselves. But the opposite is the case: *we are called to be witnesses and to bless the people of the earth*.[90]

On the one hand, it engenders deep humility and gratitude, for it excludes all boasting. On the other, it brings both peace and assurance, for nothing can quieten our fears for our own stability like the knowledge that our safety depends ultimately not on ourselves but on God's purpose of grace. Our salvation rests firmly grounded upon the historical work performed by Jesus Christ at his first appearing. ...

First, Christ abolished death. "Death" is, in fact, the one word which summarizes our human predicament as a result of sin. For death is the "wage" sin pays, its grim penalty (Rom. 6:23). And this is true of each form which death takes. For Scripture speaks of death in three ways. There is physical death, the separation of the soul from the body. There is spiritual death, the separation of the soul from God. And there is eternal death, the separation of both soul and body from God forever. All are due to sin; they are sin's terrible though just reward. But Jesus Christ "abolished" death. Neither the devil, nor our fallen nature, nor death has been annihilated. But by the power of Christ the tyranny of each has been broken, so that if we are in

Christ we can be set free. For Christians believe death is simply "falling asleep" in Jesus. ... It is the gateway to being with Christ which is far better. Spiritual death has given place to that eternal life which is communion with God begun on earth and perfected in heaven. Those in Christ will not be hurt by the second death for they have already passed out of death into life.

Secondly, Christ brought life and immortality to light through the gospel. It is through the gospel that he now reveals what he has done, and offers men the life and immortality which he has won for them. ... Such, then, is the salvation which is offered to us in the gospel and which is ours in Christ. Its character is man's re-creation and transformation into the holiness of Christ here and hereafter. Its source is God's eternal purpose of grace. Its ground is Christ's historical appearing and abolition of death.[91]

Stott had difficulty with the concept of "being saved" as only happening at the moment of a decision for Christ, as though this was all one had to do to be saved. "For it is by grace you are saved through faith – and this not from yourselves, it is the gift of God – not by works, so that no one can boast" (Eph. 2:8,9). He pointed to Philippians 2:12, "continue to work out your salvation with fear and trembling" as our present task; and to Romans 13:11, "our salvation is nearer now than when we first believed" as our future hope. Salvation is a process of past, present, and future. He affirmed these three tenses by saying:

I have been saved (in the past) from the penalty of sin by a crucified Savior. I am being saved (in the present) from the power of sin by a living Savior. And I shall be saved (in the future) from the very presence of sin by a coming Savior. ...

If therefore you were to ask me, "Are you saved?" there is only one correct answer which I could give you: "yes and no." Yes, in the sense that by the sheer grace and mercy of God through the death of Jesus Christ my Savior he has forgiven my sins, justified me and reconciled me to himself. But no, in the sense that I still have a fallen nature and live in a fallen world and have a corruptible body, and I am longing for my salvation to be brought to its triumphant completion.[92]

What then can be said about assurance of salvation? How can "once saved, always saved" and the certainty of eternal life in heaven be affirmed without being presumptuous? Stott saw the answer in his understanding of the message of St. John in his letters.

First, we know that we know Christ. Secondly, we know that we are in him and that we dwell in him and he in us. Thirdly, we know that we are of God. Fourthly, we know that we have passed from death to life and that therefore we have eternal life. To be a Christian, then, is to have been born of God, to know God and to be in him, enjoying that intimate, personal communion with him which is eternal life. John is equally at pains to show that unbelievers do not have eternal life. His purpose is to destroy the false assurance of the counterfeit as well as to confirm the right assurance of the genuine. The same two groups exist today. Some are cocksure and boast of what they may well not possess; others are conventional church goers who have no assurance of salvation, and even say it is presumptuous to claim any. There is a true Christian assurance, which is neither arrogant nor presumptuous, but is on the contrary the plainly revealed will of God for his people. Robert Law gives the three cardinal tests by which we may judge whether we possess life eternal or not. The first is theological, whether we believe that Jesus is the Son of God. The second test is moral, whether we are practicing righteousness and keeping the commandments of God. The third is social, whether we love one another. The three tests belong to each other because faith, love and holiness are all the works of the Holy Spirit.

A fresh certainty about Christ and about eternal life, based upon the grounds John gives, can still lead Christian people into that boldness of approach to God and of testimony to men, which is as sorely needed as it is sadly missing in the church today.[93]

In *Christian Basics* (1991) Stott claimed that the New Testament promised an assurance of salvation that was not incompatible with humility.

He first cites **the finished work of salvation** that Jesus Christ accomplished when he died on the cross.

Secondly he quotes **the sure word of God the Father** in 1 John 5:9,12: "We accept human testimony, but God's testimony is greater because it is the testimony of God, which he has given about his Son ... Whoever has the Son has life; whoever does not have the Son of God does not have life." God has given us two outward and visible signs of his promises in the sacraments of baptism and the Lord's Supper.

Thirdly he references **the inward witness of the Holy Spirit**. In Romans 8:16 "[T]he Spirit himself testifies with our spirit that we are God's children," especially when he prompts us to cry "*Abba*, Father" (8:15). The external witness of the Spirit is seen in our character and conduct. The chief qualities of Christlikeness are the fruit of the Spirit: love, joy, peace, patience, kindness, goodness, faithfulness, gentleness and self-control (Gal. 5:22,23).[94]

In his commentary on Titus 3:4–8, "perhaps the fullest statement of salvation in the New Testament, ... Paul isolates six ingredients of salvation – its need (why it is necessary), its source (where it originates), its ground (what it rests on), its means (how it comes to us), its goal (what it leads to) and its evidence (how it proves itself),"[95] Stott summarized:

> Its need is our sin, guilt and slavery; its source is God's gracious loving-kindness; its ground is not our merit but God's mercy in the cross; its means is the regenerating and renewing work of the Holy Spirit, signified in baptism; its goal is our final inheritance of eternal life; and its evidence is our diligent practice of good works. ...
>
> Once we have grasped the all-embracing character of this salvation, reductionist accounts of it will never satisfy us. We shall rather determine both to explore and experience for ourselves the fullness of God's salvation and to share with other people the same fullness, refusing to acquiesce, whether for ourselves or others, in any form of truncated or trivialized gospel.[96]

8

The Church

John Stott was baptized, confirmed, and ordained in the Church of England. As a child he attended All Souls Church, Langham Place where he was eventually to begin his ordained ministry and become Rector. His funeral took place there and a memorial service at St. Paul's Cathedral, London where he had been ordained in the crypt on St. Thomas Day, 21 December 1945. When he was instituted as curate (assistant minister) at All Souls after his ordination, he was required to give assent to the Thirty Nine Articles of Religion of the Church of England, adopted in 1562 to contain "the true doctrine of the Church agreeable to God's Word." He had to repeat this at his institution as Rector on 26 September 1950. On the Sunday nearest the anniversary of his institution it became his practice to read the Articles publicly, half at Morning Prayer and half at Evening Prayer, and then to preach a sermon on one of them to remind his congregation of their Protestant heritage. He believed that ignorance of the reformed doctrines of the Church of England was one of the major causes of its weakness. While he did not think the Articles were perfect, he thought that as a general statement of reformed doctrine concerning God, man, salvation, and the church they were excellent.[97]

Article XIX. *Of The Church* reads:

> The visible Church of Christ is a congregation of faithful men, in which the pure Word of God is preached, and the Sacraments ministered according to Christ's ordinance in all those things that are of necessity requisite to the same.

Article XX. *Of the Authority of the Church* reads:

> The Church hath power to decree Rites or Ceremonies, and authority in Controversies of Faith: And yet it is not lawful for the Church to ordain anything that is contrary to God's Word written, neither may it expound one place of Scripture, that it be repugnant to another. Wherefore, although the Church be a witness and a keeper of holy Writ, yet, as it ought not

to decree anything against the same, so besides the same ought it not to enforce any thing to be believed for necessity of Salvation.

The Articles present the church as under God's word written. Stott affirmed that the church is the creation of God by his Word.

> Not only has he brought it into being by his Word, but he maintains it and sustains it, directs it and sanctifies it, reforms and renews it through the same Word. The Word of God is the scepter by which Christ rules the Church and the food with which he nourishes it. This dependence of the Church on the Word is not a doctrine readily acceptable to all. In former days of Roman Catholic polemic, for example, its champions would insist that "the Church wrote the Bible" and therefore has authority over it. Still today one sometimes hears this rather simplistic argument. Now it is true, of course, that both Testaments were written within the context of the believing community, and that the substance of the New Testament in God's providence, as we have already noted, was to some extent determined by the needs of the local Christian congregations. In consequence, the Bible can neither be detached from the milieu in which it originated, nor be understood in isolation from it. Nevertheless, as Protestants have always emphasized, it is misleading to the point of inaccuracy to say that "the Church wrote the Bible"; the truth is almost the opposite, namely that "God's Word created the Church". For the people of God may be said to have come into existence when his Word came to Abraham, calling him and making a covenant with him. Similarly, it was through the apostolic preaching of God's Word in the power of the Holy Spirit on the Day of Pentecost that the people of God became the Spirit-filled Body of Christ. [*I Believe in Preaching* by John Stott. Copyright ©1982 John R.W. Stott. Reproduced by permission of Hodder and Stoughton Limited][98]

Stott did not approve of designating the day of Pentecost, in Acts 2, as the birthday of the church. The church did not begin that day. "For the church as the people of God goes back at least four thousand years to Abraham. What happened at Pentecost was that the remnant of God's people became the Spirit-filled body of Christ."[99] Commenting on Galatians 6:16, "Peace and mercy be upon all who walk by this rule, upon the Israel of God," Stott writes, "The Christian church enjoys a direct continuity with God's people in the Old Testament. Those who are in Christ today are 'the true circumcision' (Phil. 3:3), 'Abraham's offspring' (Gal. 3:29) and 'the Israel of God.'"[100] And, elsewhere he states: "So the church is God's people, His *ecclesia*, called out of the world to be His, and existing as a separate entity solely because of his call. The New Testament insists strongly upon this fact (1 Pet. 2:9,20–21; 5:10). Such is the church, God's people, called out of the world to himself, called to holiness, called to mission, called to suffering, and called through suffering to glory."[101]

Jesus uses Old Testament images of the church as God's *bride*, his *vineyard*, and his *flock*. Four principal New Testament metaphors used of the church are a *kingdom*, the sphere of God's rule, his dominion; God's *household* or family; the building God is constructing, a rebuilt *spiritual temple* with Jesus Christ as the only foundation, as witnessed by apostles and prophets, and with the Holy Spirit as the *shekinah* presence in the sanctuary; and the *body of Christ*,[102] which is why there can be no unchurched Christian, because the follower of Christ is part of the body of Christ.[103]

> For the church lies at the center of the purpose of God. God's purpose, conceived in a past eternity, being worked out in history, to be perfected in a future eternity, is not just to save isolated individuals and so perpetuate their loneliness but, rather, to call out a people for himself and to build his church. Indeed, Christ died for us not only to redeem us from sin but to purify for himself a people who are enthusiastic for good works (Titus 2:14). So, then, the reason we are committed to the church is that God is.[104]

When Stott undertook his exposition of Ephesians, which he taught in a variety of settings over a period of five years, he decided to publish it in 1979 under the title *God's New Society* in the Bible Speaks Today commentary series. He felt that one of the chief evangelical blind spots was to overlook the central importance of the church. Evangelicals proclaimed individual salvation and neglected the need for the saved community. They thought of themselves more as "Christians" than as "churchmen."[105] The true evangelical should have a very "high" view of the church. "Today, more than ever, we need to catch the biblical vision of the church."[106]

Paul understood the gospel was to "make plain to everyone the administration of this mystery, which for ages past was kept hidden in God, who created all things. His intent was that now, through the church, the manifold wisdom of God should be made known to the rulers and authorities in the heavenly realms, according to his eternal purpose that he accomplished in Christ Jesus our Lord (Eph. 3:9–11)." The biblical centrality of the church is the theme of Stott's commentary on this passage.[107] The gospel is not entirely about a personal relationship with Jesus Christ. He warned against despising the church of God and being blind to God's work in history. God has not abandoned his church. He is still building and refining it. It has a central place in his plan.

God has an eternal purpose that is being worked out in history. It concerns the church, the creating of a new and reconciled humanity in union with Jesus Christ. This is the "mystery" hidden for ages but now revealed.

Christians affirm, in contrast to all other views, that history is "his story", God's story. For God is at work, moving from a plan conceived in eternity, through a historical outworking and disclosure, to a climax within history, and then on beyond it to another eternity of the future. The Bible has this linear understanding of time. And it tells us that the center of God's eternal-historical plan is Jesus Christ, together with his redeemed and reconciled people. In order to grasp this, it may be helpful to contrast the perspective of secular historians with that of the Bible.

Secular history concentrates on kings, queens and presidents, on politicians and generals, in fact on "VIPs". The Bible concentrates rather on a group it calls "the saints", often little people, insignificant people, unimportant people, who are however at the same time God's people – and for that reason are both "unknown (to the world) and yet well-known (to God)".

Secular history concentrates on wars, battles and peace-treaties, followed by yet more wars, battles and peace-treaties. The Bible concentrates rather on the war between good and evil, on the decisive victory won by Jesus Christ over the powers of darkness, on the peace-treaty ratified by his blood, and on the sovereign proclamation of an amnesty for all rebels who will repent and believe.

Again, secular history concentrates on the changing map of the world, as one nation defeats another and annexes its territory, and on the rise and fall of empires. The Bible concentrates rather on a multi-national community called "the church", which has no territorial frontiers, which claims nothing less than the whole world for Christ, and whose empire will never come to an end.

No doubt I have painted the contrast between the secular and the biblical views of history too starkly. For the Bible does not ignore the great empires of Babylon, Egypt, Greece and Rome; and a true secular history cannot ignore the fact of the church. Yet it is a question of perspective, of priorities. The living God is the God of all the nations of the world, yet within the universal human community there exists a "covenant community", his own new society, the beginning of his new creation. It is to this people only that he has pledged himself with the everlasting promise: "I will be their God, and they shall be my people."[108]

Stott experienced the church as a covenant community – united and diverse, international, multi-racial, multi-cultural – in his travels throughout the world on every continent. No other human community resembles it. St. John described it when he explained what his proclamation of the gospel was about: "We proclaim to you what we have seen and heard, so that you may have fellowship

with us. And our fellowship is with the Father and with his Son, Jesus Christ"
(1 John 1:3).

> The purpose of the proclamation of the gospel is, therefore, not salvation
> but fellowship. Yet, properly understood, this is the meaning of salvation
> in its widest embrace, including reconciliation to God in Christ, holiness
> of life, and incorporation in the church. This fellowship is the meaning of
> eternal life. As the Son, who is that eternal life, was (eternally) with the
> Father, so he purposes that we should have fellowship with them and with
> each other. "Fellowship" is a specifically Christian word and denotes that
> common participation in the grace of God, the salvation of Christ and the
> indwelling Spirit which is the spiritual birthright of all Christian believers.
>
> This statement of the apostolic objective in the proclamation of the
> gospel, namely a human fellowship arising spontaneously from divine fel-
> lowship, is a rebuke to much of our modern evangelism and church life. We
> cannot be content with an evangelism which does not lead to the drawing of
> converts into the church, nor with a church life whose principle of cohesion
> is a superficial social camaraderie instead of a spiritual fellowship with the
> Father and with his Son Jesus Christ.[109]

After a great deal of thought and study of the biblical meaning of Christian
fellowship, the leadership of All Souls Church in London in 1965 inaugurated
the development of small Fellowship Groups. They encouraged every member
of the congregation to become a member of a group that would promote fellowship with God, care for one another, and service to the world. Members
would study the Bible but not be a Bible Study Group. They would meet every
other week for devotional Bible reading, sharing, and prayer. They would get
to know one another, love each other, take an interest in one another, and care
for each other.[110] Small groups or cell groups have become a feature of church
life today, as they were for the early Methodists in their class meetings. John
Stott personally participated in one of these groups and sought counsel of an
accountability group for guidance in his later years. He was committed to making
fellowship a reality in the church.

> I am assuming that our church is a genuine fellowship, whose members
> are bound together in mutual support and care. But all too often this kind
> of life and love is missing. Someone who drew attention to this was Dr.
> Hobart Mowrer, late Professor of Psychiatry in the University of Illinois …
> A few years ago he kindly gave time to some friends and me, who wanted
> to ask him some questions.
>
> He was not a Christian, he told us, nor even a theist. He has what
> he called "a lover's quarrel with the church". What did he mean? He

complained that the church failed him when he was a teenager, and continued to fail his parents. How so? We asked. "Because", he replied, "the church has never learned the secret of community." It is perhaps the most damaging criticism of the church which I have ever heard. For the church is community, the new community of Jesus Christ. And many churches have learned the meaning and the demands of a community of love. But others have not. [*Christian Basics* by John Stott. Copyright ©1991 John R.W. Stott. Reproduced by permission of Hodder & Stoughton][111]

In Lent 1957 Stott preached a series of sermons on Revelation 2–3 in All Souls Church, which was published the following year as *What Christ Thinks of the Church*. He identified seven marks of the true and living church, one for each of the churches addressed in the book of Revelation.

The first is *love* – a love-relationship with Jesus Christ. Theological orthodoxy without love is dead. Without love the church's work and worship is lifeless and without light and warmth.

The second is *suffering* under persecution. The temptation is to avoid suffering by compromise.

The world sees in us nothing to hate. We are seldom bold to rebuke vice. We mind our own business lest anyone be offended. We hold our tongue so that nobody is embarrassed. We are respectable, conventional, inoffensive and ineffective. The fear of man has ensnared us. We trim our sails to the prevailing theological wind. We dilute the Gospel so as to render it supposedly more palatable. We love the praise of men more than the praise of God. We escape suffering by compromise. We should not compromise on clear, moral and spiritual issues. If we do not suffer it is probably because we compromise and that if we do not compromise we certainly shall suffer.[112]

The third mark of the living church is *truth*. The central truth of the church is the doctrinal truth about Christ as the unique Son of God and his death as Savior of the world: the incarnation and the atonement.

The fourth mark is *holiness* of life, righteousness of character (1 Thess. 4:3; Eph. 1:4; Titus 2:13,14; 1 Thess. 4:7,8). "This is the balanced, joyful, exhilarating righteousness of the Bible, the glorious liberty of the royal law. It is the same morality which regards the right use of sex as beautiful and sacred, and its wrong use as ugly and sordid (Heb. 13:4)."[113]

The fifth mark is *inward reality* or authenticity as opposed to hypocrisy.

We can have a fine choir, an expensive organ, good music, great anthems and fine congregational singing. We can mouth hymns and psalms with unimpeachable elegance, while our mind wanders and our heart is far from God. We can have pomp and ceremony, color and ritual, liturgical exactness and ecclesiastical splendor, and yet be offering a worship which is not perfect or "fulfilled" in the sight of God. Those of us whose privilege it is to be in the ordained ministry can be hypocrites in our praying and preaching too. We can lead the prayers in such a perfunctory manner that the congregation never reach the throne of grace, and we can preach rather to display our learning or eloquence than to exalt Christ and bring glory to him. A torrent of words can pour from our lips, while there is neither sincerity nor power in them. Our Christian service outside church can be contaminated by the same poison. Activity with no inner love for God or man is a hollow mockery and an empty pantomime.[114]

The sixth mark of the church is *evangelism and service*. We are to go through the doors that are open to us: the doors of salvation and service in the world.

The seventh mark is *wholeheartedness*.

Our Christianity is flabby and anaemic. We appear to have taken a lukewarm bath of religion. Jesus Christ would prefer us to boil or to freeze, rather than that we should simmer down into a tasteless tepidity. Our inner spiritual fire is in constant danger of dying down. It needs to be poked and fed and fanned into flame (Rom. 12:11; Acts 18:25; 2 Tim. 1:6).

The idea of being on fire for Christ will strike some people as dangerous emotionalism. "Surely," they will say, "we are not meant to go to extremes? You are not asking us to become hot-gospel fanatics?" Fanaticism is not wholeheartedness. ... Fanaticism is an unreasoning and unintelligent wholeheartedness. It is the running away of the heart with the head. One longs today to see robust and virile men and women bringing to Jesus Christ their thoughtful and their total commitment. Jesus Christ asks for this. ... Better to be icy in my indifference or go into active opposition to him than insult him with an insipid compromise which nauseates him! Enthusiasm is an essential part of Christianity.

The tepid person is one in whom there is a glaring contrast between what he says and thinks he is in the one hand and what he really is on the other. The root cause of half-heartedness is complacency. To be lukewarm is to be blind to one's true condition. The nominal Christian is morally and spiritually a naked, blind beggar.[115]

In his analysis of John 17, "The Master's Final Prayer," at Urbana in 1970, Stott asked:

What does Christ pray for his people? What is his will for his church as revealed in his prayer? He prays that the church may be characterized by four qualities.

The first is *truth* (v.11, "Keep them in my name")

The second is *holiness* (v.15, "Keep them from the evil one" and v.17 "Sanctify them through the truth")

The third is *unity* (vv.22,23, "That they may be one ... that they may become perfectly one")

The fourth is *mission* (v.18, "I have sent them into the world" and vv.21,23, "that the world may believe").

So truth, holiness, unity and mission belong together and cannot be separated.

These are the four so-called "marks" of the church according to the Creed, namely, that the church is "one, holy, catholic [which means partly that it guards the whole truth] and apostolic [sent out into the world on a mission]."

All four are included in the prayer Jesus prayed. Most of the church's ills down the centuries and today are due to an unbalanced emphasis on one or some of these, to the neglect of others. Let's not put asunder what Christ has joined together. Let's rather pray for what he prayed and seek to secure what he prayed for – a church which guards the revelation once for all entrusted to it, a church which is sanctified and unified through this revelation which it preserves, and a church which, guarding this truth and exhibiting it in its own purity and unity, goes out on its mission to win the world for Christ.[116]

While John Stott was a member and clergyman of the Church of England all his life and urged his fellow evangelicals not to leave it when Dr. Martyn Lloyd-Jones appealed to them to do so at the National Assembly of Evangelicals in 1966, he was sympathetic to those who left the American Episcopal Church and the Canadian Anglican Church to form the Anglican Church of North America as did other mainline churches such as the Presbyterians. He enumerated five situations when orthodox believers might feel obliged to leave.

First, when an issue of first order is at stake, such as deserves the condemnation "antichrist" (1 John 2:22) or "anathema" (Gal. 1:8,9).

Secondly, when the offending issue is held not by an idiosyncratic minority of individuals but has become the official position of the majority.

Thirdly, when the majority have silenced the faithful remnant, forbidding them to witness or protest any longer.

Fourthly, when we have conscientiously explored every possible alternative.

Fifthly, when after a painful period of prayer and discussion, our conscience can bear the weight no longer.[117]

He went on the record to say that "if the church were officially to approve homosexual partnerships as a legitimate alternative to heterosexual marriage, this so far diverges from biblical sexual ethics that I would find it exceedingly difficult to stay. I would have to leave."[118]

On the 150th anniversary of the dedication of All Souls Church in 1974, John Stott concluded a sermon (with apologies to Martin Luther King) with his dream for the future of the church.

I have a dream of a church that is a *biblical church* – which is loyal in every particular to the revelation of God in Scripture, whose pastors expound Scripture with integrity and relevance, and so seek to present every member mature in Christ, whose people love the word of God, and adorn it with an obedient and Christ-like life, which is preserved from all unbiblical emphases, whose whole life manifests the health and beauty of biblical balance.

I have a dream of a church which is a *worshipping church* – whose people come together to meet God and worship him, who know God is always in their midst and who bow down before him in great humility, who regularly frequent the table of the Lord Jesus, to celebrate his mighty act of redemption on the cross, who enrich the worship with their musical skills, who believe in prayer and lay hold of God in prayer, whose worship is expressed not only in Sunday services and prayer gatherings only but also in their homes, their weekday work and the common things of life.

I have a dream of a church which is a *caring church* – whose congregation is drawn from many races, nations, ages and social backgrounds, and exhibits the unity and diversity of the family of God, whose fellowship is warm and welcoming, and never marred by anger, selfishness, jealousy or pride, whose members love one another with a pure heart fervently, forbearing one another, forgiving one another, and bearing one another's burdens, which offers friendship to the lonely, support to the weak, and acceptance of those who are despised and rejected by society, whose love spills over to the world outside, attractive, infectious, irresistible, the love of God himself.

I have a dream of a church which is a *serving church* – which has seen Christ as the Servant and has heard his call to be a servant too, which is delivered from self-interest, turned inside out, and giving itself selflessly to the service of others, whose members obey Christ's command to live in the world, to permeate secular society, to be the salt of the earth and the light of the world, whose people share the good news of Jesus simply, naturally and enthusiastically with their friends, which diligently serves its own parish, residents and workers, families and single people, nationals and immigrants, old folk and little children, which is alert to the changing needs of society, sensitive and flexible enough to keep adapting its program to serve more usefully, which has a global vision and is constantly challenging its young people to give their lives in service, and constantly sending its people out to serve.

I have a dream of a church which is an *expectant church* – whose members can never settle down in material affluence or comfort, because they remember that they are strangers and pilgrims on earth, which is all the more faithful and active because it is waiting and looking for its Lord to return, which keeps the flame of the Christian hope burning brightly in a dark despairing world, which on the day of Christ will not shrink from him in shame, but rise up joyfully to greet him.[119]

9

Preaching

In 1961 John Stott gave the Payton Lectures at Fuller Theological Seminary in Pasadena, California. Later that year they were published as *The Preacher's Portrait: some New Testament word studies.* His five chapters were divided as follows:

1. ***The Preacher as Steward: his message and authority*** (1 Cor. 4:1,2). The steward is not the owner but the trustee and dispenser of another's person's goods. The preacher is not at liberty to create and share thoughts or convictions of his own. Preaching is not a matter of propagating one's own opinions. Instead, the preacher is a steward of God's mysteries, that is, of the self-revelation God has entrusted to us, and which is now preserved in the Scriptures. The stewardship metaphor indicates the content of the preacher's message. The preacher does not supply his own message; he is supplied with it. Our task is "setting forth the truth plainly" (2 Cor. 4:2). This is a good definition of preaching. Preaching is a spoken manifestation of the truth that stands written in the Scriptures.

   Therefore, every sermon should be, in some sense, an expository sermon. The preacher may use illustrations from political, ethical, and social fields to illumine and enforce the biblical principles he is seeking to unfold, but the pulpit is no place for purely political commentary, ethical exhortation or social debate. We are to preach "the word of God", and nothing else (Col. 1:25).

   Moreover, we are called to preach the whole range of the Word of God (Acts 20:27). ... How few preachers could advance the same claim! Most of us ride a few of our favorite hobby-horses to death. We pick and choose from the Scriptures, selecting doctrines we like and passing over those we dislike or find difficult. ... Some not only subtract from, but add to the Scriptures while others presume to contradict what stands written in God's Word.[120]

Stott would work through books of the Bible, e.g. Galatians, the Pastoral Epistles; and selected chapters such as the ones on the Sermon on the Mount, or on the fruit of the Spirit; and occasional courses of sermons to cover all aspects of the gospel and the Christian life. Apart from the chief festivals of the Christian year and Holy Week he did not follow the lectionary. He was not tied to liturgical and ecclesiastical directions but gave himself to expounding every part of the New Testament. He rarely preached on the Old Testament (except the Psalms) since his expertise was in New Testament Greek and not in Hebrew. This required him to plan his series of sermons many months in advance, and advertise them. He respected the ability of his listeners to absorb what he had to offer as God's word to them. He was neither too brief in his exposition nor too long, exhausting their concentration, but took into consideration their needs.

> The wise steward varies the diet which he gives to the household. He studies their needs and uses his discretion in supplying them with suitable food. ... It is not enough for the preacher to know the Word of God; he must know the people to whom he proclaims it. ... he may seek to present it to the people in such a way as to commend it to them. For one thing, he will make it simple. ... The expository preacher is a bridge-builder, seeking to span the gulf between the Word of God and the mind of man.[121]

2. *The Preacher as Herald: his proclamation and appeal* (1 Cor. 1:21,23). The herald proclaims good news to the world. He announces God's supernatural intervention. His proclamation issues an appeal and expects a response. Through the herald's proclamation God in Christ directly confronts people with himself. The content of his proclamation in the Acts of the Apostles is the work of Christ, which proves Jesus as both Lord and Savior, requiring the hearers to repent and receive the forgiveness of sins (1 Cor. 1:23; 2 Cor. 4:5). This is the irreducible minimum of the gospel. "We preach Christ crucified" is the heart of the gospel. We also preach Christ's life, resurrection, and exaltation. "But the emphasis in the New Testament *kerygma* is on the Savior's atoning death for the sins of the world."[122] This leads to an appeal to come to Christ in repentance and faith.

> True evangelism seeks a response. It expects results. It is preaching for a verdict. Heralding is not the same as lecturing. A lecture is dispassionate, objective, academic. It is addressed to the mind. It seeks no result but to impart certain information and, perhaps, to provoke the student to further enquiry. But the herald of God comes with an urgent proclamation of peace through the blood of the Cross, and with a summons to men to repent, to lay down their arms and humbly to accept the offered pardon.[123]

Preaching that leaves the hearers with no opportunity to respond and concludes with a lame affirmation in the name of the Trinity or some other ascription, may be teaching but it is not heralding. It is like reading a menu but providing no food to nourish and satisfy.

The herald is also an ambassador, a term used by Paul in 2 Corinthians 5:18–21 to describe the role of the preacher. "All this is from God" (2 Cor. 5:18). God is the author of reconciliation. Stott quotes William Temple: "All is of God. The only thing of my very own which I contribute to my redemption is the sin from which I need to be redeemed."

God made Christ to be sin with our sins, so that we might become righteous with his righteousness. This mysterious exchange is possible only to those who are "in him" who are personally united to Christ by faith. God was in Christ to achieve our reconciliation; we must be in Christ to receive it. ... It is this reconciliation which we are called to proclaim as heralds. God has made Christ to be sin for us. This is the "gospel" of which we are heralds. It is the proclamation of a fact, of a deed which is gloriously done and absolutely finished, of a gift which may now be freely received.[124]

We are ambassadors for Christ, God making his appeal through us. Stott references Paul's ministry in Ephesus, where he argued daily in the hall of Tyrannus for two years – a daily five-hour proclamation amounting to 25,000 hours of gospel preaching. If preachers were to follow his example they would not be afraid to teach people solid doctrine or to reason with them.

The great lesson the herald metaphor can teach us, as it is used in the New Testament, is that proclamation and appeal belong together. We must not separate them.

First, we must never issue an appeal without first making the proclamation. The gospel is not fundamentally an invitation to do anything. It is a declaration of what God has done in Christ on the cross for their salvation. The invitation cannot properly be given before the declaration has been made. Men must grasp the truth before they are asked to respond to it. The apostles ... sought to make an intellectual conquest, to persuade men of the truth of their message, to convince them in order to convert them. ...

Secondly, we must never make the proclamation without then issuing an appeal. ... It is not enough to teach the gospel; we must urge men to embrace it.[125]

Thy heralds brought glad tidings
To greatest, as to least;
They bade men rise and hasten
To share the great king's feast ...

Their gospel of redemption,
Sin pardoned, man restored,
Was all in this enfolded:
One Church, one faith, one Lord.[126]

3. ***The Preacher as Witness: his experience and humility*** (Acts 20:21,24; John 15:26,27). "Jesus Christ stands on trial at the bar of world opinion. Secular, godless, non-Christian society, now uncommitted, now hostile, is in the role of judge. The devil accuses him with many ugly lies. The Holy Spirit is the counsel for the defense. He calls us to be witnesses to substantiate his case."[127] Christian preachers testify for Christ, defending and commending him to the world. The world is sometimes apathetic and indifferent, and sometimes aggressive and rebellious. The preacher is called to give witness against an unbelieving world's opposition to Christ. "Christian witness is testimony to Jesus (Acts 4:33). So much so-called testimony today is really autobiography and even sometimes thinly disguised self-advertisement."[128]

The preacher's witness is drawn from the Scripture and inspired by the Spirit. The witness must have a personal experience, first-hand knowledge of Jesus Christ. It cannot be second-hand or from hearsay.

Our task is not to lecture about Jesus with philosophical detachment. We have become personally involved in him. His revelation and redemption have changed our lives. Our eyes have been opened to see him, and our ears unstopped to hear him, as our Savior and Lord. "It is quite futile saying to people 'Go to the Cross.' We must be able to say 'Come to the Cross.' And there are only two voices which can issue that invitation with effect. One is the voice of the Sinless Redeemer, with which we cannot speak; the other is the voice of the forgiven sinner, who knows himself forgiven. That is our part." (William Temple)[129]

There is no greater need for the preacher than that he should know God. I care not about his lack of eloquence and artistry, about his ill-constructed discourse or his poorly enunciated message, if only it is evident that God is a reality to him and that he has learned to abide in Christ. The preparation of the heart is of far greater importance than the preparation of the sermon. The preacher's words, however clear and forceful, will not ring true unless he speaks from conviction born of experience. Many sermons which conform to all the best homiletical rules, yet have a hollow sound. There is something indefinably perfunctory about the preacher. The matter of his sermon gives evidence of a well-stocked, well-disciplined mind; he has a good voice, a fine bearing, and restrained gestures; but somehow his heart is not in his message. ... The preaching of a witness has a spontaneity about it, and infectious warmth, a simply directness, a depth of reality, which are all due to an intimate knowledge of God. So we must hunger and thirst after him. ... We shall remember that the real preparation of a sermon is not the few hours which are specifically devoted to it, but the whole stream of the preacher's experience thus far, of which the sermon is a distilled drop. As E.M. Bounds has put it, "the man, the whole man, lies behind the sermon. Preaching is not the performance of an hour. It is the outflow of a life. It takes twenty years to make a sermon, because it takes twenty years to make a man."[130]

The witness should not draw attention to himself but to Christ. Stott described the painting by William Westall that hangs on the east wall of All Souls Church above the communion table. It measures about 12 x 9 feet and dominates the interior of the church. It was presented by King George IV when the church was consecrated in 1824.

It depicts the Lord Jesus, manacled but majestic, surrounded by evil-looking priests and coarse soldiers who mock at him. All round his head are the hands of these men, pointing to the object of their derision. I see in this picture a symbol of our ministry. Jesus Christ is the center of our message. We are but signposts pointing to him. What those soldiers and priests in the picture do in scorn and hatred we do in love and worship. And the more our vision is filled with him, the less shall we lapse into self-centered vanity.[131]

4. *The Preacher as Father: his love and gentleness* (1 Cor. 4:14–21; 1 Thess. 2:11,12). Love is the chief quality of a father. How does this express itself in the preaching ministry?

First, a father's love will make us understanding in our approach. The people of the congregation to whom we preach have many problems, intellectual, moral, personal, domestic. Stott claimed that too much preaching is academic or theoretical. The preacher talks abstractly in generalities about Christian virtues but does not deal with specifics. You can accurately expound a passage of Scripture without relating it to actual human needs. A father should understand his children as they are developing. He cares about them and tries to enter into their hopes and fears, their weaknesses and difficulties. Too many fathers are detached and indifferent to their children and fail to be sensitive to their needs. Fathers can ignore them as they throw themselves into their own work and leisure pursuits. They can neglect their children at a time when they need them most. The preacher should never be like this. He takes the time and trouble to discover what their problems are if he loves them. The challenge for the preacher is that he can live a different life from his congregation. He sees his members when they need him, in hospital or in a crisis, but not in their everyday lives. He likely has not experienced the stress and competition of business life and can be suspicious, unsympathetic, and critical of career advancement and the pursuit of profits. He may not have had to work with his hands and endure long hours on the job under the supervision of officious managers. The preacher may be more familiar with mental work at his own pace. This may be why many business and working men are not found in great numbers in churches: perhaps they find the preaching irrelevant to their daily lives. Teachers, social and psychological workers are more likely to be drawn to churches than laborers, business and professional men. Perhaps the preacher talks glibly about the Christian life and witness but is unrealistic about the challenges people face. Perhaps he advances his own political opinions and proposes solutions to the world's problems, which he knows nothing about, dismissing the possibility that he may be mistaken and at variance with his hearers' convictions and experience.

It really is of the greatest importance that we think ourselves into the situation in which our people find themselves; that we identify ourselves with them in their sorrows, responsibilities and perplexities; and that we do not live, or appear to them to live, in a remote ivory tower. Such an estrangement between preacher and congregation is most harmful to the proclamation and to the reception of the message. Speakers and hearers are not on the same wave-length.

How can we effect a rapprochement? Read books, magazines, and news-papers. Listen to people as we meet with them. Love will help the preacher to be understanding in his approach not only because he will then take the trouble to get to know his people and their problems, but also because he will be the better able to appreciate them when he knows them. ... Love, the unselfish care which longs to understand and so to help, is one of the greatest secrets of communication. It is when the preacher loves his people, that they are likely to say of him, "He understands us".[132]

Secondly, a father's love will make us gentle in our manner. "So many of us are naturally brusque and rough-handed. By temperament we are neither meek nor sensitive. Yet the true father, whatever his character may be like and however strict a disciplinarian he may be, shows a certain tenderness towards his children. His love makes him gentle (Matt. 11:29; 2 Cor. 10:1; 1 Thess. 2:7; 2 Tim. 2:24,25)." Stott pointed out the tragedy of a preacher becoming sour, disappointed, frustrated, and with few visible results becoming embittered. Early enthusiasm and zeal is dashed, and the preacher turns to sarcasm, expressing self-pity and conceit. Love does not descend into giving vent to bitterness. True parents never want to shame their children, but encourage them and affirm them. "Dr. Parker repeated again and again, 'Preach to broken hearts!' And here is the testimony of Ian Maclaren: 'The chief end of preaching is comfort.' Dr. Dale, 'People want to be comforted. They need consolation – really need it, and do not merely long for it.'"[133]

Thirdly, a father's love will make us simple in our teaching. "With what patient simplicity does a father spell out the alphabet to his child! He humbles himself to the child's level. ... If we love them, our objective will not be to impress them with our learning, but to help them with theirs. To make easy things hard is everyman's work; but to make hard things easy is the work of a great preacher" (James Ussher).[134] Stott held up Billy Graham's preaching as an example of simplicity and directness. He did not assume that his hearers are familiar with the Scriptures and Christian doctrines and did not talk over their heads. Too many preachers think that all in the congregation are college graduates with majors in theology and philosophy.

Simplicity in preaching begin with our subject-matter. We shall need to spend most of our time expounding the central themes of the gospel; the more abstruse matters of prophecy, and questions of controversial or speculative character we can well afford to leave on one side. ... To a simple subject and a simple style add simple words. And we must keep clear of jargon. If we are wise, we shall take nothing for granted. Use pictorial language to visualize what we are talking about. Then let us not be afraid of appealing to people's power of imagination.[135]

Fourthly, a father's love will make us earnest in our appeal. A father who loves, cares; and a father who cares will not hesitate to use entreaty if he has cause for anxiety about his children. Just as the father warns his children of danger, the faithful preacher will sometimes preach of sin, judgment and hell. It is no mark of love to leave them alone in their peril (1 Thess. 1:10). "The true function of the preacher is to disturb the comfortable and to comfort the disturbed" (Chad Walsh). ...

We have already thought about men's need of comfort, as there is so much to disturb us in these days. But there are others who are not disturbed when they should be. They are self-satisfied and self-sufficient. They feel no need for God and have no thought of judgment and eternal destiny. Can we abandon them in their fool's paradise? ... we shall preach it in love, for we dare not preach such things with callous harshness or unfeeling nonchalance. And if we preach in love, the people will pay attention.[136]

Fifthly, a father's love will make us consistent in our example (1 Pet. 5:2,3). "A practical doctrine must be practically preached. We must study as hard how to live well as how to preach well" (Richard Baxter).[137]

Sixthly, a father's love will make us conscientious in our prayers. A devoted father prays for his children daily. We must pray for those to whom we preach. Praying and preaching go hand in hand. This is the balanced ministry to "give our attention to prayer and the ministry of the word" (Acts 6:4).

5. *The Preacher as Servant: his power and motive* (1 Cor. 3:5). Stott was concerned with the cult of personality in the pulpit. With the advent of television this has become even more prevalent. Even local pastors love to hear their sermon commended by their parishioners as they greet people at the end of the service. Flattery is a great danger. Too many people go to church to hear a man rather than worship God or to hear his Word. Many charlatans are great orators but manipulate their hearers with their rhetoric. Sermons are not meant to be "enjoyed."

A sermon is never an end in itself, but a means to an end, the end being "saving souls" (Phillip Brooks). I have no hesitation in saying that people who "congratulate" a preacher on his sermon, and preachers who expect such congratulation from their people are alike most offensive to God. Men are called to preach not themselves but Christ Jesus as Savior and Lord (1 Cor. 1:23; 2 Cor. 4:5). What matters, therefore is Christ himself who is proclaimed, and not the men who proclaim him. To think or act otherwise is not only to usurp God's glory, but to jeopardize the preacher's whole ministry, bringing it first into discredit and finally to ruin.

The Corinthians attached too much importance to their favorite preachers. We are mere servants, Paul asserts, servants of Jesus the Lord, and what glory is due to servants? We are "servants through whom you believed, as the Lord assigned to each" (1 Cor. 3:5), and having stated this, Paul enlarges on the correct view of the Christian ministry throughout this and the following chapters of his Epistle.[138]

Stott called attention to the urgent and indispensable need for God's power in preaching. He saw in the older, historic churches few signs of life or power. The depraved human condition will not be affected by mere human enlightenment or persuasion. Unredeemed men and women are sightless and lifeless, blind and dead (Eph. 2:1; 4:18). How can preachers become channels of God's power as to be "servants through whom" others will believe? Preachers should read and study 1 Corinthians 1:17–2:5 rather than rely on other people to judge and reform their ministry.

Where is God's power to be found?

> First, there is power in the Word of God. Our task as Christian preachers is not to subserviently answer all the questions which men put to us; nor to attempt to meet all the demands which are made on us; nor hesitantly to make tentative suggestions to the philosophically minded; but rather to proclaim a message which is dogmatic because it is divine. The preacher's responsibility is proclamation not discussion. "If any one among you thinks that he is wise in this age, let him become a fool that he may become wise" (1 Cor. 3:18). I believe that this "let him become a fool" is one of the hardest words of Scripture to the proud hearts and minds of men. Like the brilliant intellectuals of ancient Greece our contemporaries have unbounded confidence in the human reason. They want to think their way to God by themselves, and to gain credit for discovering God by their own effort. But God resists such swelling of pride on the part of the finite creature.

> Secondly, there is power in the cross of Christ. What offends the proud, saves the humble. There is wonderful power in the cross of Christ. It has power to wake the dullest conscience and melt the hardest heart; to cleanse the unclean; to reconcile him who is far off and restore him to fellowship with God; to redeem the prisoner from his bondage and lift the pauper from the dunghill; to break down the barriers which divide men from one another; to transform our wayward characters into the image of Christ and finally make us fit to stand in white robes before the throne of God.

> Thirdly, there is power in the Holy Spirit (1 Thess. 1:5). Every preacher who has been endowed with gifts of personality and fluent speech knows the temptation to put his confidence in the power of his own ability. Only the Holy Spirit can convict the conscience, illumine the mind, enflame the heart and move the will.[139]

Charles Spurgeon used to say to himself as he mounted the steps to his pulpit: "I believe in the Holy Ghost, I believe in the Holy Ghost, I believe in the Holy Ghost." Stott often quoted Spurgeon writing: "the power that is in the gospel does not lie in the eloquence of the preacher; otherwise men would be converter of souls. Nor does it lie in the preacher's learning; otherwise it would consist in the wisdom of men. We might preach till our tongues rotted, till we should exhaust our lungs and die, but never a soul would be converted unless there were mysterious power going with it – the Holy Ghost changing the will of man."[140]

Stott believed that there were two essential conditions for the preacher to become a channel of God's power: holiness and humility. Paul came to Corinth in weakness and in much fear and trembling. His human weakness was a necessary condition to receiving divine power (2 Cor. 12:7–10).

> I cannot help wondering if this may not be why there are so few preachers whom God is using today. There are plenty of popular preachers, but not many powerful ones, who preach in the power of the Spirit. Is it because the cost of such preaching is too great? It seems that the only preaching God honors, through which his wisdom and power are expressed, is the preaching of a man who is willing in himself to be both a weakling and a fool. We are constantly tempted to covet a reputation as men of learning or men of influence; to seek honor in academic circles and compromise our old-fashioned message in order to do so; and to cultivate personal charm or forcefulness so as to sway the people committed to our care. So let preacher and congregation humble themselves, willing to be despised as both weak and foolish, in order that all the wisdom and power of salvation may be ascribed where they belong, namely to the three glorious Persons of the eternal Trinity.[141]

Stott was not interested in methodology, the techniques that some homiletic department of seminaries taught. He was a convictional preacher.

> In other words, theology is more important than methodology. By stating the matter thus bluntly, I am not despising homiletics as a topic for study in seminaries, but rather affirming that homiletics belongs properly to the department of practical theology and cannot be taught without a solid theological foundation. To be sure, there are principles of preaching to be learned, and a practice to be developed, but it is easy to put too much confidence in these. Technique can only make us orators; if we want to be preachers, theology is what we need. If our theology is right, then we have all the basic insights we need into what we ought to be doing, and all the incentives we need to induce us to do it faithfully. [*I Believe in Preaching* by John Stott. Copyright ©1982 John R.W. Stott. Reproduced by permission of Hodder and Stoughton Limited][142]

He claimed that expository preaching is extremely rare today. He set himself the task to convince his readers of the necessity of conscientious biblical preaching; he gave five theological convictions that should underlie the preacher's work:

First there is *a conviction about God*. "The kind of God we believe in determines the kind of sermons we preach."[143] God is light and wants to shine his light into the darkness in which people find themselves. God has acted to reveal himself in redemptive activities to rescue us. God has spoken both through historical deeds and explanatory words. He has spoken through the prophets, through the Word made flesh, and through the apostles.

Secondly, there is *a conviction about Scripture*. It is God's word written (see Article 20 of the Anglican Thirty Nine Articles of Religion). The divine speech has been committed to writing. God put his word into human minds so that his words were theirs as well. "Inspiration was not in any way incompatible with either their historical researches or the free use of their minds."[144] Stott affirmed Scripture's human as well as its divine authorship. "The New Testament authors were writing as theologians, each of whom selected and presented his material according to his particular theological purpose."[145] God still speaks through what he has spoken. God's voice is not silent today. The Holy Spirit speaks through the word of God. Therefore, God's word is powerful. It is sharper than any two-edged sword; it is a hammer, a fire, a lamp, a mirror, a seed, milk, wheat, honey, and gold (Heb. 4:12; Jer. 23:29; Ps. 119:105; Jas. 1:18,22–25; 1 Pet. 1:23–2:2; Ps. 19:10).

Thirdly, there is *a conviction about the church*. "The word of God is the scepter by which Christ rules the church and the food with which he nourishes it."[146] A major reason for the church's decline is what Amos called a "famine of hearing the words of the Lord" (8:11). "The low level of Christian living is due, more than anything else, to the low level of Christian preaching."[147]

Fourthly, there is *a conviction about the pastorate*. Pastors are to feed their flock, i.e. teach them. Stott quoted Michael Ramsey: "The priest is the teacher and preacher, and as such he is the *man of theology*. He is pledged to be a dedicated student of theology; and his study need not be vast in extent but it will be deep in its integrity, not in order that he may be erudite, but in order that he may be simple. It is those whose studies are shallow who are confused and confusing."[148] The essential nature of the pastorate is the ministry of the Word and prayer (Acts 6:4). But some members of the flock can be unteachable. I, for example, remember how a prominent member of one of my congregations came to me and said, "You don't think that you can teach us anything, do you?"

Fifthly, there is *a conviction about preaching*. What sort of sermons should we preach? There are topical sermons and textual sermons. There are evangelistic or prophetic, doctrinal or ethical, and devotional sermons. Expositional sermons are more than a verse-by-verse explanation of a lengthy passage of Scripture, such as I heard recently by a man who used every verse as an opportunity to declaim on a different subject, so that he preached several sermons in one, and left his hearers exhausted. Expository preaching is not a running commentary on a passage.

> The expositor prizes open what appears to be closed, makes plain what is obscure, unravels what is knotted and unfolds what is tightly packed. The opposite of exposition is 'imposition', which is to impose on the text what is not there. ... In expository preaching the biblical text is neither a conventional introduction to a sermon on a largely different theme, nor a convenient peg on which to hang a ragbag of miscellaneous thoughts, but a master which dictates and controls what is said. [*I Believe in Preaching* by John Stott. Copyright ©1982 John R.W. Stott. Reproduced by permission of Hodder and Stoughton Limited][149]

The preacher should not go off at a tangent and follow his own fancy, or strain or stretch the text into something quite different from its original and natural meaning. Too often preachers have chosen texts as pegs on which to hang their thoughts and have wrenched them out of their context.[150] Stott quoted his mentor, Charles Simeon, on integrity in preaching:

> Be most solicitous to ascertain from the original and from the context the true, faithful and primary meaning of every text ... I endeavor without prejudice or partiality, to give to every text its just meaning, its natural bearing and its legitimate use ... to bring out of Scripture what is there, and not to thrust in what I think might be there. I have a great jealousy on this head: never to speak more or less than I believe to be the mind of the Spirit in the passage I am expounding.[151]

John Stott's *I Believe in Preaching* was published in London in 1982; it was published in the same year in the United States as *Between Two Worlds: the art of preaching in the twentieth century*.[152] In his Introduction, Stott thanked me for challenging him to relate the gospel to the modern world. As I was ministering to students, I was acutely aware of the issues they were preoccupied with, which caused me to question him after one of his sermons: "So what?" What was the application of his biblical message to the contemporary world? After he retired in 1975 from being Rector of All Souls Church, he founded the London Institute for Contemporary Christianity to foster relating the world of the Bible to the world of today.

Those two "worlds" is what the title of his American edition referred to: preaching is a bridge-building exercise between the world of the Bible and the world of today.

In *The Contemporary Christian*, Stott addressed the question of how to apply God's word to the concerns of the present time:

I believe we are called to the difficult and even painful task of "double listening". That is, we are to listen carefully (although with differing degrees of respect) both to the ancient word and to the modern world, in order to relate the one to the other with a combination of fidelity and sensitivity. Every chapter is, in fact, an attempt at double listening, although I am sure that some are much less successful than others. It is, however, my firm conviction, that, only if we can develop our capacity for double listening, will we avoid the opposite pitfalls of unfaithfulness and irrelevance, and be able to speak God's word to God's world with effectiveness today.[153]

It requires entering into the worlds of thought and feeling of our contemporaries, Stott urged preachers. It is incarnational: the eternal entering into the temporal, relating the word to the world or Christ to the individual. It means dealing with the major themes of human life, the questions raised in literature and history: What is the purpose of our existence? Has life any significance? Where did I come from, and where am I going to? What does it mean to be a human being, and how do humans differ from animals? From where is this thirst for transcendence, this universal quest for a Reality above and beyond us, this need to fall down and worship the Infinitely Great? What is freedom, and how can we experience personal liberation? Why the painful tension between what I am and what I long to be? Is there a way to be rid of guilt and of a guilty conscience? What about the hunger for love, sexual fulfilment, marriage, family life, and community on the one hand, and on the other the pervasive sense of alienation, and the base, destructive passions of jealousy, malice, hate, lust, and revenge? Is it possible to truly master oneself and love one's neighbor? Is there any light on the dark mysteries of evil and suffering? How can we find courage to face first life, then death, then what may lie beyond death? What hope can sustain us in the midst of our despair?[154]

If we believe that the gospel of Christ is the answer to these questions, we must preach Christ, the contemporary Christ. The riches of Christ are unfathomable (Eph. 3:8, NEB).

> To encounter Christ is to touch reality and experience transcendence. He gives us a sense of self-worth or personal significance, because he assures us of God's love for us. He sets us free from guilt because he died for us, from the prison of our self-centeredness by the power of his resurrection, and from paralyzing fear because he reigns, all the principalities and powers of evil having been put under his feet. He gives meaning to marriage and home, work and leisure, personhood and citizenship. He introduces us into his new community, the new humanity he is creating. He challenges us to go out into some segment of the world which does not acknowledge him, there

to give ourselves to witness and service for him. He promises us that history
is neither meaningless nor endless, for one day he will return to terminate
it, to destroy death and to usher in the new universe of righteousness and
peace. "In him (Christ) the whole fullness of deity dwells bodily, and you
have come to fullness of life in him." (Col. 2:9,10) One of the most fasci-
nating of all the preacher's tasks is to explore both the emptiness of fallen
man and the fullness of Jesus Christ, in order then to demonstrate how he
can fill our emptiness, lighten our darkness, enrich our poverty, and bring
our human aspirations to fulfillment. The riches of Christ are unfathomable.
[*I Believe in Preaching* by John Stott. Copyright ©1982 John R.W. Stott.
Reproduced by permission of Hodder and Stoughton Limited][155]

Stott also raised the situations of social injustice that cry out for political solutions. In many Christian pulpits they are the subjects of contemporary sermons
by preachers who are wanting to appear relevant. They include the problems
of racism, inequality, tribalism, poverty, climate change, and many others. They
are debated continually in our media and in our universities. We cannot ignore
them. We cannot divorce the Christian faith from Christian life and encourage a
pietistic withdrawal from the world. If we are to preach the Bible we must take
note of its prophetic concern for justice and compassion.

I am not suggesting that the pulpit is the place in which precise political
programs are framed or from which they are commended. Rather it is the
preacher's responsibility to open up the biblical principles which relate to
the problems of contemporary society, in such a way as to help everybody
to develop a Christian judgment about them, and to inspire and encourage
the opinion-formers and policy-makers in the congregation, who occupy
influential positions in public life, to apply these biblical principles to their
professional life. ... The pulpit should help them to develop their Christian
thinking and so to penetrate their segment of the human community more
deeply for Christ. [*I Believe in Preaching*. Copyright ©1982 John R.W.
Stott. Reproduced by permission of Hodder and Stoughton Limited][156]

He emphasized that avoidance of these problems is not possible. Partisanship
is not desirable. The preacher is not to ventilate private opinions. To be dogmatic on social and political issues where there are differences of opinions among
Christians is foolish.

Is there a way to handle controversial topics in the pulpit which is brave not
cowardly, humble not dogmatic, and prudent not foolish? I think there is.
It is to help Christians to develop a Christian mind. The Christian mind ...
is not a mind which is thinking about specifically Christian or even religious
topics, but a mind which is thinking about everything, however apparently

"secular", and doing so "Christianly" or within a Christian frame of reference. It is not a mind stuffed full with pat answers to every question, all neatly filed as in the memory bank of a computer; it is rather a mind which has absorbed biblical truths and Christian presuppositions so thoroughly that it is able to view every issue from a Christian perspective and so reach a Christian judgment about it. ... Christians should facilitate the recovery of the lost Christian mind. For by our systematic exposition of the Bible over the years we should be giving our congregation a framework of truth. This will include such basic convictions as the reality and loving personality of the living God, the dignity of human beings by creation and their depravity by the fall, the pervasiveness of evil and the primacy of love, the victory and reign of Christ, the centrality of the new community in God's historical purpose, the transience of time and the certainty of the *eschaton* of judgment and salvation. More simply, a mind may be said to be Christian when it has firmly grasped the fourfold biblical scheme of creation, fall, redemption, and consummation, and is able to evaluate the phenomena of life in the light of it. So all our preaching, week in and week out, should gradually unfold "the whole counsel of God" and so contribute to the development of Christian minds in the congregation.

How, then, does this task relate to controversial preaching? How can we help church members to think Christianly about a particular topic of debate? It seems that we have a fourfold duty. First, we must expound with courage, clarity, and conviction the biblical principle or principles which are involved, and those aspects of the subject on which God has plainly revealed his will. Secondly, we should seek to summarize fairly the alternative applications which biblical Christians have made, and the arguments they have used to buttress their conclusions. Thirdly, we should feel free, if we judge it wise, to indicate which position we hold and why. And fourthly, we should leave the congregation free, after grasping the principles we have taught and weighing the issues we have sketched, to make up their own minds. [*I Believe in Preaching* by John Stott. Copyright ©1982 John R.W. Stott. Reproduced by permission of Hodder and Stoughton Limited][157]

The teacher must handle difficult issues, which may divide his congregation, with respect, Stott cautions. It is a challenge to preach with the authority of God's word while at the same time respecting the mind and will of the hearers. We are called not to coerce our listeners but instead to ask for a thoughtful, loving, and free response. This is how Paul dealt with the issue of what Christians should eat (Rom. 14:14,15). The strong should bear with the failings of the weak and stop passing judgment on one another (Rom. 14:13; 15:1). We should not jump onto the latest bandwagon of the news cycle and virtue-signal by trumpeting the strident voices of the spirit of the age.

> We who are called to be Christian preachers today should do all we can to help the congregation to grow out of dependence on borrowed slogans and ill-considered clichés, and instead to develop their powers of intellectual and moral criticism, that is, their ability to distinguish between truth and error, good and evil. Of course, we should encourage an attitude of humble submission to Scripture, but at the same time make it clear that we claim no infallibility for our interpretations of Scripture. We should urge our hearers to "test" and "evaluate" our teaching. We should welcome questions, not resent them. We should not want people to be moonstruck by our preaching, to hang spellbound on our words, or to soak them up like sponges…
>
> In conclusion, let me summarize the principal features of a preaching ministry which is conceived as an activity of bridgebuilding between the revealed Word and the contemporary world. Such preaching will be authoritative in expounding biblical principles, but tentative in applying them to the complex issues of the day. This combination of the authoritative and the tentative, the dogmatic and the agnostic, conviction and open-mindedness, teaching the people and leaving them free to make up their own minds, is exceedingly difficult to maintain. But it seems to me to be the only way on the one hand to handle the word of God with integrity (declaring what is plain, but not pretending that everything is plain when it is not) and on the other to lead the people of God into maturity (by encouraging them to develop a Christian mind, and use it). [*I Believe in Preaching* by John Stott. Copyright ©1982 John R.W. Stott. Reproduced by permission of Hodder and Stoughton Limited][158]

On the occasion on his 70th birthday, Stott wrote an article for the *All Souls Magazine* entitled "People Who Have Influenced Me." He mentioned seven of them, including me:

> His great concern in preaching was to relate the Gospel to the issues of the day, while sometimes (I thought) being a bit slapdash in his biblical exegesis. My great concern on the other hand, was to expound Scripture faithfully, while sometimes (he thought) neglecting its contemporary application. On Monday mornings we would compare notes. I would tell him how I thought he could strengthen his exposition, and he would tell me how I could strengthen my application. If only we could combine forces, we said to one another, building on our strength and overcoming our weakness. So Ted was without doubt one of those whose influence lay behind the concern to relate the word to the world, and so behind the founding of the London Institute for Contemporary Christianity in 1982.

10

The Sacraments

What Christ said about the Scriptures is equally true of the sacraments, namely Baptism and the Lord's Supper. Their function and purpose are the same. Both the Scriptures and sacraments are God-given signposts (the Scriptures in written words, the sacraments in visible words or pictures) directing our attention away from themselves to Christ. Verbally in Scripture, visually in sacrament, Jesus Christ is set forth as the only Savior of sinners. But neither Scripture nor sacrament is an end in itself. Both are means to an end, namely that we find salvation (understood in its full New Testament sense) in Christ. Thus both are means of *grace*, media through which God's grace is offered to us, because they exhibit Christ to us and kindle our faith in Him. Indeed, "the sacraments function as a means of *grace* because, and only because, God uses them, as He uses His Word as a means to *faith*" (J.I. Packer). So the evangelical should steadfastly repudiate any *ex opere operato* view of either Scripture or sacrament. Neither the reading of the Bible, nor the receiving of Baptism or Holy Communion brings any automatic blessing. God's Word read and preached does not benefit a congregation unless it "meets with faith in the hearers" (Heb. 4:2). Nor are the sacraments beneficial to the unbelieving. Since they are "visible words", they also must be met with faith. Indeed, "in such only as worthily receive the same they have a wholesome effect or operation" (Art. XXV). And "worthy" reception means believing reception.[159]

Stott followed the teaching of the Articles of Religion about the Sacraments. Article XXV: Of the Sacraments, states that they are "certain sure witnesses, and effectual signs of grace, and God's good will towards us, by the which he doth work invisibly in us, and doth not only quicken, but also strengthen and confirm our Faith in him."

The same Article states, "There are two Sacraments ordained of Christ … in the Gospel: Baptism and the Supper of the Lord." At the Reformation it was concluded the other "five commonly called Sacraments, that is to say, Confirmation, Penance, Holy Orders, Matrimony and Extreme Unction, are not to be counted for Sacraments of the Gospel ... for they have not any visible sign or ceremony ordained of God."

Holy Baptism

What follows in this section I paraphrased mainly from *The Anglican Evangelical Doctrine of Infant Baptism*.[160]

Both sacraments of the gospel are sacraments of grace, that is, sacraments of divine initiative, not of human activity. The candidate of baptism never baptizes himself, but always submits to being baptized by another. He is the passive recipient of something that is done to him. As Augustus Toplady wrote in his famous hymn, "Rock of Ages":

> *Nothing in my hand I bring,*
> *simply to thy cross I cling;*
> *naked come to thee for dress,*
> *helpless look to thee for grace;*
> *foul I to the fountain fly;*
> *wash me, Savior, or I die.*

Articles 25, 27 and 28 all begin with the statement that a sacrament is a sign not of what we do or are, but of what God has done, or does. That is why the current practice of processing with the elements of bread and wine as an offering contradicts the theology of God supplying the body and blood of Christ.

Baptism signifies three things.

First of all, it signifies **union with Christ** (Rom. 6:3). While baptism is into the one name of the three Persons of the Trinity (Matt. 28:19), in Acts and the Epistles it is in the name of Jesus – because it is he who revealed the Father and sent the Holy Spirit, so that we cannot be related to him without being related to them also. This union with Christ signifies participation into his death and the power of his resurrection, the end (by death or burial) of the old life of sin, and the beginning (by resurrection or birth) of the new life of righteousness. This is the controlling idea in baptism.[161]

Secondly, baptism signifies **the forgiveness of sins** (Acts 2:38; 22:16). This was the emphasis of John the Baptist.

Thirdly, baptism signifies **the gift of the Spirit**. John the Baptist said, "I baptize you with water ... He will baptize you with the Holy Spirit" (Matt. 3:11). But water baptism continued by the command of Christ so that it now intended to signify the very Spirit-baptism with which it had previously been contrasted. The pouring of water dramatizes the outpouring of the Holy Spirit by which he promised we would be baptized. Jesus said, "Whoever believes in me … rivers of living water will flow from within them. By this he meant the Spirit, whom those who believed in him were later to receive" (John 7:38,39).

"Baptism is to be understood as an eschatological sacrament, inasmuch it initiates into the New Covenant which belongs to the New Age. It does this by incorporating us into Christ, for Jesus Christ is the mediator of the New Covenant, and the bestower of its blessings."[162] Incorporation into Christ includes incorporation into the Body of Christ. The Article XXVII, Of Baptism states: "Baptism is … a sign of Regeneration or new Birth, whereby, as by an instrument, they that receive Baptism rightly are grafted into the Church; the promises of forgiveness of sin, and our adoption to be the sons of God by the Holy Ghost, are visibly signed and sealed; Faith is confirmed, and Grace increased by virtue of prayer unto God."

What is the effect of baptism?

The evangelical view is that the outward and visible sign not only signifies the gift but seals it and pledges it in such a way as to convey not the gift itself, but a title to the gift. The view of baptismal regeneration that all who are baptized are born again flies in the face of reality. There is a difference between the visible and the invisible church. It is possible to belong to a visible church without belonging to the Body of Christ, which is invisible in the sense that its members are known to God alone (2 Tim. 2:19). "Many within are without; and some without are within."[163] The visible church consists of the baptized, while the invisible church consists of the regenerate. Simon Magus is an example of someone who was baptized, but he was not right with God (Acts 8:13–24).

Article 27 speaks of receiving baptism *rightly*.

That means to receive it with faith. Abraham was justified by faith and was circumcised as the sign or seal of the covenant (Rom. 4:11). What circumcision was to Abraham and his descendants, baptism is to us (Rom. 2:28,29; Col. 2:10–13). It is not only the sign of covenant membership, but a seal or pledge of covenant blessings. Baptism does not convey these blessings to us but conveys to us a right or title to them, so that if and when we truly believe, we inherit the blessings to which baptism has entitled us. Just as a will gives an estate to a beneficiary, it does not take effect until the death of the testator. To truly believing adults the covenant sign of baptism (like circumcision to Abraham) signifies and seals a grace that they have already received by faith. To the infant child of believing parents, the covenant sign of baptism (like to Isaac at the age of eight days) is administered because they are born into the covenant and are thereby "holy" in status (1 Cor. 7:14), but it signifies and seals to them graces that they still need to receive later by faith. Their baptism as infants conveyed to them a title to the blessings of the new covenant they inherit when they exercise their faith. They do not need to be rebaptized when they believe. Since a sacrament is a visible word, and it is the function of God's word to arouse faith (Rom. 10:17), the sacraments stimulate our faith to lay hold of the blessings they signify and to which they entitle us. The gift is not tied to the time of the sacrament's administration. It is possible to receive the sign before the gift, as is usual in the case of infants, or to receive the sign after the gift, as is usual in the case of adults.

> People need to be warned, for the good of their soul, that the reception of the sign, although it entitles them to the gift, does not convey the gift to them. They need to be taught the indispensable necessity of personal repentance and faith if they are to receive the thing signified. Our task is to be faithful in teaching the significance of baptism and the conditions of its efficacy; and then not to baptize any but those who profess to be penitent believers, and their children (Acts 2:38,39).[164]

Holy Communion

There are three Articles devoted to the Lord's Supper. Article XXVIII reads as follows:

> The Supper of the Lord is not only a sign of the love that Christians ought to have among themselves one to another; but rather is a Sacrament of our Redemption by Christ's death; insomuch that to such as rightly, worthily, and with faith, receive the same, the Bread which we break is a partaking of the Body of Christ; and likewise the Cup of Blessing is a partaking of the Blood of Christ.
>
> Transubstantiation (or the change of the substance of Bread and Wine) in the Supper of the Lord, cannot be proved by holy Writ; but is repugnant to the plain words of Scripture, overthroweth the nature of a Sacrament, and hath given occasion to many superstititions.
>
> The Body of Christ is given, taken, and eaten, in the Supper, only after an heavenly and spiritual manner. And the means whereby the Body of Christ is received and eaten in the supper is Faith.
>
> The Sacrament of the Lord's Supper was not by Christ's ordinance reserved, carried about, lifted up, or worshipped.

Stott deals with the Lord's Supper at length in his 1958 book *Your Confirmation*, which was reissued as *Christian Basics* in 1991. The following is an outline of his interpretation of the meaning of the sacrament.

First, it is a service of remembrance. Jesus instituted it by saying "Do this, whenever you drink it, in remembrance of me" (1 Cor. 11:23–25). The simplest and most obvious meaning of the Lord's Supper is that it commemorates the death of Jesus Christ on the cross. He was drawing attention to his death and its purpose. Stott goes on to quote the third exhortation in the 1662 Anglican service: "To the end we should always remember the exceeding great love of our Master and only Savior Jesus Christ, thus dying for us, and the innumerable benefits which by his precious blood-shedding he obtained to us; he hath instituted and ordained holy mysteries, as pledges of his love, and for a continual remembrance of his death, to our great and endless comfort."[165] In order to stimulate our minds and memories, the officiating minister both copies the actions and repeats the words of Jesus in the upper room.

Secondly, it is a service of participation. Jesus did more than take and break bread, and take and pour wine, saying "this is my body, this is my blood"; he also gave the elements to the apostles, saying "take, eat and drink." Thus they were not only spectators of the drama (watching and listening), but participants in it (eating and drinking). The Lord's Supper is more than a "commemoration," by which we recall an event of the past; it is a "communion," by which we share in its present benefits. This was Paul's emphasis when he wrote: "Is not the cup of thanksgiving for which we give thanks a participation in the blood of Christ? And is not the bread that we break a participation in the body of Christ?" (1 Cor. 10:16). Two questions now confront us. In what do we actually participate? How do we participate in it?

In what according to God's purpose do we participate at the Lord's Supper? The answer must be "the body and blood of Christ." But what does this mean? It means the death of Jesus Christ, together with the benefits he obtained for us by his death. The "body and blood of Christ" is a figure of speech for the benefits of his death, not for the power of his life.

How do we participate in Christ's body and blood? If it is not by eating and drinking that we receive Christ (the Roman Catholic and Lutheran position), how is it? It is by faith, of which eating and drinking are a vivid picture. For just as by eating the bread and drinking the wine we take them into our bodies and assimilate them, so by faith we feed on Christ crucified in our hearts and make him our own. Article

28 states that those who "rightly, worthily, and with faith" receive the sacrament also partake of Christ's body and blood, and that "the means whereby the Body of Christ is received and eaten in the Supper is Faith." Similarly, the famous sixteenth-century Anglican theologian Richard Hooker wrote: "The real presence of Christ's most blessed body and blood is not to be sought for in the sacrament, but in the worthy receiver of the sacrament." This is why the Anglican doctrine is sometimes called "Receptionism."

The sacraments have been given to stimulate our faith. In fact, they are means of grace mainly because they are means to faith. And the Lord's Supper is a means to faith because it sets forth in dramatic visual symbolism the good news that Christ died for our sins in order that we might be forgiven. Hugh Latimer, the great preacher of the English Reformation, explained this symbolism during his trial in Oxford, before going to the stake: "There is a change in the bread and wine, and such a change as no power but the omnipotency of God can make, in that that which before was bread should now have the dignity to exhibit Christ's body. And yet the bread is still bread, and the wine is still wine. For the change is not in the nature but the dignity."[166] This is sometimes called "transignification," in distinction to "transubstantiation," for the change in mind is one of significance not of substance. As the officiant offers the bread and wine to our bodies, so Christ offers his body and blood to our souls. As we take the bread and wine and feed on them in our mouths by eating and drinking, so we feed on Christ crucified in our hearts by faith.

Thirdly, it is a service of fellowship. During the Reformation, the Altar was replaced by the Lord's Table and brought down into the body of the church so that the congregation could gather around it. Paul wrote, "Because there is one loaf, we, who are many, are one body, for we all partake of the one loaf" (1 Cor. 10:17). To retain this vivid symbolism, real bread should be used rather than wafers. Each communicant receives a fragment from the same loaf, because each is a member of the same body, the body of Christ, the church. Further, since the loaf is an emblem of our crucified Savior, it is our common participation in him (set forth visibly in our common participation in it) that makes us one.

The Lord's Supper, which is the church's fellowship meal on earth, is also a foretaste of the heavenly feast. Paul tells us that whenever we eat the bread and drink the cup, we "proclaim the Lord's death until he comes" (1 Cor. 11:26). For when he comes, he will consummate his kingdom, and the symbol will give way to the reality.

Fourthly, it is a service of thanksgiving. "Eucharist" (*eucharistia* being the Greek word for thanksgiving) was from the very early days a name for the Lord's Supper. The focus of our thanksgiving should be God's wonderful love for us in the death of his Son in our place and in the salvation he has procured for us in consequence. It is in this sense that the Lord's Supper is, or rather includes, a "sacrifice." We ask God to accept our sacrifice of praise and thanksgiving.

What is meant, then, by "eucharistic sacrifice"?

The traditional Catholic answer is that it is an offering of Christ to God. This notion, that on the altar at mass Christ is offered to God as a propitiatory sacrifice for sins, was rejected by the Reformers, who were determined to go back to Scripture. They saw the Catholic mass as derogatory to the unique and wholly satisfactory sacrifice of Christ on the cross. So, in order to be consistent, they carefully avoided every use of the word "altar" and replaced it with "the Holy Table," "the Lord's Table" or simply "the Table." For they saw the officiant at Communion not as a priest sacrificing at an altar, but as a minister serving at a table. He administers a sacrament to the people; he does not offer a sacrifice to God. We participate in Christ's sacrifice only in the sense that we share in the benefits of it, not in the sense that we share in the offering of it.

What then is the relation between Christ's sacrifice and us?

It is multiple. We remember his sacrifice with adoring gratitude. We partake by faith of its saving benefits. We enjoy with one another the fellowship it has made possible. And we offer ourselves to God in responsive self-sacrifice. But we do not and cannot share in Christ's offering of himself. To suggest this is to confuse what must be kept distinct, namely his offering and ours, "the perfect and the tainted, the atoning and the Eucharistic, the divine initiative and the human response."[167]

11

Mission

In 1967 Stott published *Our Guilty Silence*, which presented the primary responsibility of the church as making known the gospel of Christ and winning others to him. It challenged the church to recover its evangelistic vision and to embark afresh on its evangelistic mission. "If the gospel is the good news it claims to be, and if it has been entrusted to us, we incur guilt if we do not pass it on."[168] He believed that there were four major causes of our guilty silence. "Either we have no impelling incentive even to try to speak, or we do not know what to say, or we are not convinced that it is our job, or we do not believe we shall do any good, because we have forgotten the source of power."[169] He addressed each of these causes by providing their antidotes.

He argued that the Christian is motivated by obedience to Christ and compassion for the lost. He is also motivated by jealousy for God, whose glory he gives to no other. He tells the story of Henry Martyn, the friend of his mentor Charles Simeon. In 1805 Martyn went out as a missionary to India and then to Persia. He moved to Shiraz and busied himself with the translation of the New Testament into Persian. Many Muslim visitors came to see him and to engage him in religious conversation. His customary serenity was only disturbed when anybody insulted his Lord. On one occasion the sentiment was expressed that "Prince Abbas Mirza had killed so many Christians that Christ from the fourth heaven took hold of Mahomet's skirt to entreat him to desist." It was a dramatic fantasy. Here was Christ kneeling before Mahommed. How would Martyn react? "I was cut to the soul at this blasphemy." Seeing his discomfiture, his visitor asked what it was that was so offensive. Martyn replied: "I could not endure existence if Jesus was not glorified; it would be hell to me, if he were to be always thus dishonored." His Muslim visitor was astonished and again asked why. "If anyone pluck out your eyes," he answered, "there is no saying why you feel pain; it is feeling. It is because I am one with Christ that I am thus dreadfully wounded." Stott commented:

I never read these words of Martyn's without being rebuked, for I do not have this passionate love for Christ's honor or felt this acute pain. Nor do I see it much (if at all) in the contemporary church. But is not this the cause of our guilty silence? We do not speak for Christ because we do not so love his name that we cannot bear to see him unacknowledged or unadorned. If only our eyes were opened to see his glory, and if only we felt wounded by the shame of his public humiliation among men, we should not be able to remain silent. Rather we would echo the apostles' words: "we cannot but speak of what we have seen and heard" (Acts 4:20).[170]

He goes on to give the second reason for our guilty silence being "that we are neither clear nor sure what we ought to speak. We lack either a thorough knowledge of the Gospel or a conviction about its truth or both. This has never been more apparent than it is today. Theological indecision is an obvious feature of contemporary Christendom. The chief cause of this dilemma is the rapidity with which modern life is changing."[171]

The gospel is about Christ, who came to save us. And his salvation is a comprehensive deliverance from all sin. It begins with our forgiveness and our reconciliation with God. It continues with our progressive liberation from the down-drag of indwelling sin and with our transformation into the image of Christ. It will be consummated at Christ's return when we are given new bodies in a new world, from which all sin has been forever excluded.

It is tragic beyond words that this high and holy purpose of God to save men through Christ has been frequently diluted by the church. Instead of the faithful proclamation of this good news, evangelism becomes a pathetic exhortation to bad men to be good and (more often) supposedly good men to be better, or an attempt to induce people to come to church to worship.[172]

The three major constituents of the gospel of God are: Jesus Christ and him crucified, the plight and peril of man in sin and under judgment, and the necessary response called the "obedience of faith." This is the irreducible minimum.

To promote evangelism in his own congregation Stott established an Annual Training School of twelve weekly lectures on the theology of the gospel and the practice of evangelism. At the end there was an examination and a commissioning of lay workers. He held a guest service once a month and encouraged church members to bring a relative, friend, colleague or neighbor to hear the gospel and hopefully respond to the invitation to commitment at the close.

What is the point of evangelism?

In 2 Corinthians 4:4–6 the apostle Paul describes in graphic terms both the condition of the unconverted and the marvel of conversion. Preaching the gospel is the divinely appointed means by which the devil's power in men's lives is overthrown and God shines savingly into their hearts. Stott concluded that, "Our greatest need in evangelism today is the humility to let God be God. Our motive must be concern for the glory of God."[173]

Eight years later in *Christian Mission in the Modern World*[174] Stott expressed himself differently. While maintaining the priority of evangelism, he wrote that social responsibility was among the things Jesus commanded: "The actual commission itself must be understood to include social as well as evangelistic responsibility, unless we are to be guilty of distorting the words of Jesus."[175] Stott went on to develop the relationship between evangelism and social action.

The theme of the Urbana Conference of 1976 was "Declare His Glory Among the Nations." Participating were missionaries from India, Ecuador, Zaire, Costa Rica, and Colombia; evangelists from Uganda, Argentina, and the United States; pastors from India, Canada, London, and Mississippi; students from North America; student workers from Singapore, the Philippines, Canada, and the United States; a music director from Canada; and a variety of widely read authors. They learned that 2.7 billion people in the world had never heard the message of salvation through Jesus Christ. Some 8,529 students signed World Evangelism Decision Cards indicating their willingness to go wherever God might choose to send them.

John Stott gave the Bible Studies on "The Biblical Basis of Missions." His purpose was to convince his hearers that world mission was a central feature of the historical purpose of God according to Scripture and is a responsibility he lays upon all his people. In 1992 this series of expositions was republished as Chapter 19 in *The Contemporary Christian*. Stott examined the four major sections into which the Bible is divided: Old Testament, Gospels, Acts, and Letters.[176]

The first exposition was entitled "The Living God is a Missionary God." The Old Testament basis for mission was to be found in the call to Abraham (Gen. 11:31–12:4). God made a promise to bless Abraham, to make him a great nation, to make his name great, to bless him so that he would be a blessing to all the families of the earth. The whole of God's purpose is encapsulated in this promise. The context of this promise is that God is the Creator of the heavens and the earth. Therefore, his call to Abraham is a universal call, not confined to Israel. He is the one God, not a tribal god. "Monotheism lies at the basis of mission."[177] This one God made all people. Yet the first chapters of Genesis chronicles moral deterioration, darkness, and dispersal. Society steadily disintegrated. Yet God did not abandon the human beings he made in his own likeness. He chose Abraham in order to call people back to himself.

God promised that Abraham ("father of a multitude") would become the father of a multitude of nations. His descendants would become as numerous as the stars in the sky and the grains of sand on the seashore. He promised that he would be given a new homeland in a new country. He promised that his blessing would spill over upon all humanity. He established an everlasting covenant with Abraham, signified by circumcision. This promise was fulfilled in the life of the nation of Israel, in Christ and his church, and ultimately it would be fulfilled in the new heaven and the new earth (Heb. 11:12). Matthew traces the beginning of the gospel of Jesus Christ to Abraham. His spiritual descendants would inherit the promise (Matt. 8:11–12). Peter applied the promise to all who would repent and believe in Jesus (Acts 3:25–26). Paul saw the fulfillment in terms of the Gentiles (Rom. 9:6–7). In Romans 4, Paul claimed that neither physical descent from Abraham, nor physical circumcision as a Jew, makes a person a true child of Abraham but only faith (Gal. 3:6–9). The blessing is that of salvation. "If you belong to Christ, you are Abraham's seed, and heirs according to the promise" (Gal. 3:29). The final fulfillment is the vision in Revelation of "the great multitude which no man can number" before the throne of God (Rev. 7:9ff.). They are countless as the stars in the sky and the sand on the seashore, composed of people from every nation.

God is the God of history. He is working out in time a plan in which Jesus Christ as the seed of Abraham is the key figure. We, if we are Christ's disciples, are Abraham's descendants and are beneficiaries of the promise made to Abraham. God is the God of blessing. God is the God of mercy who saves not a few people but a great multitude. God is the God of mission who blesses the world through Abraham's seed by faith. He is the God of all the families of the earth, whatever race or culture.

The second exposition was entitled "The Lord Christ is a Missionary Christ." The Great Commission has five versions. The most pregnant and the most neglected is John 20:19–23. The essence of Christ's message is "I send you" (v.21). Jesus possesses universal authority to send all his disciples into the world. The nature of the mission is, first of all, peace (v.19). There is peace of mind, which dispelled their doubts and reassured them. There is peace of conscience for their sense of guilt at abandoning him. By showing them his hands and his side he was assuring them of forgiveness. There is peace in the church, for we all need reconciliation, racial and social, in our fellowship.

Christ's summons to mission is, "As the Father has sent me, even so I send you." Our mission is to be like his. "He has sent me to proclaim freedom for the prisoners," echoes the words of Isaiah (Luke 4:18). Christ was sent to preach the good news of the kingdom of God (Luke 4:43) and he was deeply aware of being sent. "It gave significance, urgency and compulsion to everything he did."[178] This is part of the very nature of the church. Christ's mission was compassionate. He was moved with compassion by the needs of the crowds. So must we be. Humanity's most fundamental need is salvation; but we have no right to limit our mission to evangelism alone. Christian evangelistic and social activity are both compassionate responses to human need.

Christ's mission was costly. By his incarnation he made himself vulnerable to pain, weakness, poverty, sorrow, suffering, and temptation. Jesus was not aloof. He did not keep his distance from sinners; he was the friend of sinners. He touched the untouchable lepers and allowed prostitutes to touch him; he shrank from nobody. His death on the cross was the ultimate identification with us in our sins. Jesus calls us to apply to our mission in the world the same principles that characterized his mission. The most Christian context in which to offer service and share the gospel is genuine, caring friendship. We need to translate the gospel not only into the languages of the world but also into the cultures of the world. We are called to incarnation evangelism: we have to listen, to enter into the other person's thought world, to try to understand their misunderstandings, their hangups, problems, doubts, and fears.

Jesus breathed on the disciples and said to them, "Receive the Holy Spirit" (v.22). They needed the power of the Holy Spirit if they were to succeed in their mission. The presence and power of Christ to be received at Pentecost was anticipated in his words and action.

The message of Christ's mission was forgiveness (v.23). Jesus was giving them the commission to preach the gospel. If you repent and believe, your sins will be forgiven; if you refuse, they will not be forgiven. He was sending them out into the world from behind the closed doors of the Upper Room. He sends us out also from the closed doors of our churches and fellowships to share the gospel.

The third exposition was entitled "The Holy Spirit is a Missionary Spirit" (Acts 2:1–47).

First of all, there is the promise of the Spirit (in Acts 1). The main topics of our Lord's instruction during the 40 days between his resurrection and his ascension concerned the kingdom of God and the Spirit of God. The apostles misunderstood the nature of the kingdom. Jesus had to correct their understanding by teaching them that God's kingdom is spiritual in character: it is the reign of God in the lives of his people; it is his divine rule in human hearts and lives in the power of the Spirit;

it is not purely internal experience in our hearts, for it has external consequences in the way we live.

God's kingdom is also international in its membership. It would extend beyond Israel to Samaria and then to the ends of the earth (Acts 1:8). Luke writes about the expansion of the kingdom of God to Rome. Within about thirty years a small Jewish sect became a cosmopolitan Christian community. The barriers between race, color, nation, and tribe are broken down.

God's kingdom is gradual in its expansion. The whole period between Christ's ascension and Christ's return was to be filled with the Christian missionary enterprise. Christians are to be witnesses to the end of the age. Only when the gospel has been preached to all nations will the end come (Matt. 24:14).

Secondly, Luke describes the coming of the Spirit on the day of Pentecost (in Acts 2:1–41). He lists fifteen areas around the Mediterranean from which the hearers of the gospel came. This is a reversal of the confusion of the Tower of Babel. Peter explains what had happened, beginning with Jesus. His first word is "Jesus" and it must be ours as well. Jesus is the heart and soul of the good news. But which Jesus did Peter proclaim? He preached the objective Jesus of history and of Scripture rather than the subjective Jesus of experience or speculation. Peter summarized the saving career of Jesus: he was a historical figure wonderfully attested by God with signs and wonders; he was crucified by the wickedness of men and for the purpose of God; God had raised him from the dead as the prophets foretold and exalted him to his right hand to be both Lord and Christ; from that position of supreme honor and executive power Jesus had poured out the promised Holy Spirit. Those who hear must repent and be baptized in the name of Jesus Christ to receive the forgiveness of sins and the gift of the Holy Spirit.

Thirdly, Luke describes the community of the Spirit (in Acts 2:42–47). The church multiplied in one day twenty-six times, growing from 120 people to 3,120. It was a learning community. The Spirit taught them through the Old Testament Scriptures supplemented by the apostles' teaching. The apostles' teaching is now found in the New Testament Scriptures. The new believers devoted themselves to the fellowship of the Spirit, a fellowship that involved generosity, reciprocal meeting of needs, and worship. They became generous stewards of what they had, met the needs of one another, and devoted themselves to the celebration of the Lord's Supper and to prayer. Worship was both formal and informal, in the temple and in their homes, and it was both joyful and reverent. The Lord added to their number day by day those who were being saved. The Holy Spirit was reaching out through and beyond the church to those still outside its fellowship. Evangelism was the work of the Holy Spirit bringing people into the church continually. "Apostolic instruction, fellowship, worship, evangelism were and still are marks of the Spirit's presence and are what people are looking for in the contemporary church."[179]

The fourth exposition was entitled "The Christian Church is a Missionary Church." The church itself is seen in the Epistles to be God's new society: a new community, the new creation of God. The very existence of the church in the first century, with the new life its members were living, was a testimony to the saving power of God's gospel. In 1 Peter 2:1–12 we find one of the fullest and most vivid characterizations of the church to be found in the New Testament. Peter brings together five striking metaphors to illustrate different aspects of the church's being and consequent responsibility.

First, the church is likened to newborn babies. Peter wants them to grow up into maturity. They do it by drinking the pure spiritual milk of the word of God. The daily discipline of Scripture meditation is necessary if we are to grow into maturity in Christ.

Secondly, the church is living stones built upon the foundation of Jesus Christ. We are to be built into a spiritual house, attached to one another to form a solid community of faith, hope, and love.

Thirdly, the church is holy priests who offer spiritual sacrifices acceptable to God through Jesus Christ. All of us enjoy direct access to God through Jesus Christ to offer our "sacrifices" of praise. We are a priesthood of all believers in touch with the transcendent God.

Fourthly, the church is a chosen people, a holy nation, a people belonging to God, to declare the wonderful deeds of him who called us out of darkness into his marvelous light. This is an echo of Exodus 19:4–6 and Deuteronomy 7:6. We are the true Israel, God's chosen, holy, priestly, special people, his peculiar treasure. God has elected us to witness to him, to be a light to the nations (Isa. 4:1,6). We witness to deliverance from the darkness of sin and guilt, the darkness of ignorance and death. God has enlightened us, adopted us, had mercy on us.

Fifthly, the church is a community of aliens and exiles. We have been born again into God's family and kingdom. Heaven has become our home. Therefore, we are strangers, even refugees, on earth. We are citizens of two kingdoms and we have responsibilities to perform in both. Earthly possessions, affluence, luxuries, sorrow, suffering, and death all look quite different in the light of eternity. Holiness or Christlike character becomes important to us only when we remember that we are traveling to an eternal destiny. Christlike character endures. We have important duties on earth, but we must never allow them to preoccupy us in such a way that we forget who we are and where we are heading. We are not to behave like a secular humanist who believes that man is on his own and that this life is everything. We have a more exciting and enduring life in Christ to bear witness to.

Chapter 20 of *The Contemporary Christian* is entitled "Holistic Mission," and here we see how Stott's thinking on the subject developed from the Lausanne Covenant of 1974 to the 1982 Lausanne Consultation on the Relationship between Evangelism and Social Responsibility held in Grand Rapids, where he stated that,

> Evangelism relates to people's eternal destiny and, in bringing them good news of salvation, Christians are doing what nobody else can do. Seldom if ever should we have to choose between ... healing bodies and saving souls. ... Nevertheless, if we must choose, then we have to say that the supreme and ultimate need of all humankind is the saving grace of Jesus Christ, and that therefore a person's eternal, spiritual salvation is of greater importance than his or her temporal and material well-being.[180]

According to Stott, social action not only follows evangelism as its consequence and aim, and precedes it as its bridge, but also accompanies it as its partner. They are like two blades of a pair of scissors, or like two wings of a bird. It is how they were in the public ministry of Jesus. The partnership is in reality a "marriage." All followers of Jesus Christ have the responsibility, according to the opportunities given them, both to witness and to serve. Mission describes everything the church is sent into the world to do, namely Christian service in the world comprising both evangelism and social action. Each missionary must be true to his or her particular calling. Some are called to primary evangelism, and some are called to educational, medical or social work.

> The biblical basis for this partnership is to be found, first, in ***the character of God*** who is both Creator and Redeemer. He calls all people to repent and believe. He also cares for the poor and the hungry, the alien, the widow, and the orphan. He denounces oppression and tyranny, and calls for justice. The two great commandments are to love God and love our neighbor.

> Secondly, it is to be found in ***the ministry and teaching of Jesus***. Words and work went together in his public ministry. He went about preaching, and

doing good and healing. His words explained his works; and his works dramatized his words. In the parables of the Prodigal Son and the Good Samaritan there is a portrayal of a victim, of himself, and of others. There is also a rescue. In both cases love triumphs over prejudice. By contrast the elder brother, and the priest and Levite refuse to get involved. Stott cites the example of General William Booth, the founder of the Salvation Army, who said that it was no use just preaching the gospel and leaving people in their misery.

Thirdly, the biblical argument for the partnership of evangelism and social action concerns *the communication of the gospel*. Verbal communication is not enough. The Word became flesh. We cannot announce God's love with credibility unless we exhibit it in action. Good news and good works are inseparable. Stott considered five objections to this partnership:

1. *Shouldn't Christians steer clear of politics?* Social service may be acceptable, but social action involves politics. If political action can be defined as love seeking justice for the oppressed, then it is a legitimate extrapolation from the biblical emphasis on the practical priorities of love.

2. *Isn't this going back to the old social gospel?* The social gospel attempted to identify the kingdom of God with socialized society. It was a self-confident utopianism. The social implications of the biblical gospel are different. We are called to be the salt of the earth and the light of the world.

3. *Isn't this social concern the same as liberation theology?* No, for we are not equating social, economic and political liberation with salvation. We do not endorse Marxist theories and methods, or espouse violence. Total liberation of human beings from everything that oppresses, demeans or dehumanizes them is surely pleasing to God. But material liberation is not "salvation" in the biblical sense.

4. *Isn't it impossible to expect social change unless people are converted?* No, it isn't. Jesus Christ through his people has had an enormous influence for good on society as a whole. He quotes Martin Luther King: "Morality cannot be legislated, but behavior can be regulated. Judicial decrees may not change the heart, but they can restrict the heartless. ... The law cannot make an employer love me, but it can keep him from refusing to hire me because of the color of my skin."[181]

5. *Won't commitment to social action distract us from evangelism?* It need not. We should be grateful to evangelical watchdogs who bark loud and

long if they see any signs in us of a diminished commitment to evangelism. Social action, far from diverting us from evangelism, will make it more effective by rendering the gospel more visible and credible.

Such an "evangelical watchdog" was Arthur Johnston, who in his book, *Battle for World Evangelism*, was critical of the Lausanne Covenant in general and John Stott in particular. He urged vigilance against liberals, was totally negative about the ecumenical movement, and claimed that Stott had dethroned evangelism as the only historical aim of mission. Stott replied in an article in *Christianity Today* that he had attempted to enthrone love as the essential historical motivation for mission. "If we see our brothers or sisters in need (whether spiritual or social), and have the wherewithal to meet their need, but fail to do so, how can we claim that God's love dwells within us?" He asserted that evangelicals have had their blind spots, for example, on slavery and race, and therefore need to express penitence.[182]

Stott concluded his discussion of mission in *The Contemporary Christian* in Chapter 21, "The Christology of Mission":

Let me recapitulate what Christ's saving career says to us about mission. The *model* for mission is his incarnation (identification without loss of identity), its *cost* is his cross (the seed which dies multiplies), its *mandate* is his resurrection (all authority is now his), its *motivation* is his exaltation (the honor of his name), its *power* is his gift of the Spirit (who is the paramount witness), and its *urgency* is his Parousia (we will have to give him an account when he comes).

It seems to me that the church needs to keep returning, for its inspiration and direction, to this Christological basis of mission. ... If only we could gain a fresh and compelling vision of Jesus Christ, incarnate and crucified, risen and reigning, bestowing the Spirit and coming again! Then we would have the clarity of purpose and strength of motive, the courage, the authority, the power and the passion for world evangelization in our time. John Venn described a missionary in the following terms. His eloquent portrait is equally applicable to every kind of Christian witness: "*With the world under his feet, with heaven in his eye, with the gospel in his hand and Christ in his heart, he pleads as an ambassador for God, knowing nothing but Jesus Christ, enjoying nothing but the conversion of sinners, hoping for nothing but the promotion of the kingdom of Christ, and glorying in nothing but in the cross of Jesus Christ, by which he is crucified to the world, and the world to him.*"[183]

Stott was extremely conscious of the missionary challenge of bridging the two worlds of the Bible and contemporary culture. He was affected by the spectacle of African Christians who interpreted their faith in terms of European culture (Gothic church buildings and Tudor clerical robes and language) rather than their indigenous culture. He was sensitive to the criticism of Southern-hemisphere Christian leaders that American and European missionaries expected them to conform to their cultural understanding of the Christian life. In his booklet *Culture and the Bible*, Stott asks, "Why do people reject the gospel that missionaries bring?" and suggests in answer: "Often it is not because they think it to be false, but either because they perceive it as a threat to their own culture or because it is presented to them in terms of a foreign culture."[184]

The Lausanne Consultation on Gospel and Culture held at Willowbank, Bermuda, 7–9 January 1978, brought 33 theologians, anthropologists, linguists, missionaries, and pastors together from all six continents. John Stott was the Chairman, who, together with Robert Coote, edited the seventeen papers subsequently published in 1979 under the title *Down to Earth: studies in Christianity and culture*. It quoted the Willowbank Report that addressed the problem of the gospel being presented to people in alien cultural forms.

> Then the missionaries are resented and their message rejected because their work is seen not as an attempt to evangelize but as an attempt to impose their own customs and way of life. Where missionaries bring with them foreign ways of thinking and behaving, or attitudes of racial superiority, paternalism, or preoccupation with material things, effective communication will be precluded. Sometimes, these two cultural blunders are committed together, and messengers of the gospel are guilty of cultural imperialism which both undermines the local culture unnecessarily and seeks to impose an alien culture instead.[185]

Section 6 of the Report is entitled, "Wanted: Humble Messengers of the Gospel!" The Incarnation is the model for Christian witness where the Son of God "made himself nothing by taking the very nature of a servant, being made in human likeness. And being found in appearance as a man, he humbled himself and became obedient to death – even death on a cross!" (Phil. 2:7,8). Missionaries, whether in the same culture or across cultures, have the challenge of appreciating the culture of their hearers and learning to communicate relevantly within that context. This requires great humility, skillful listening, and a commitment to learning. "There is an urgent need today for creative Christian thinkers who will be utterly loyal to the essentials of the biblical gospel, but who will express it in fresh ways appropriate to every culture. To this task the Incarnation commits us."[186]

In his Foreword to *Down to Earth*, John Stott wrote,

The major challenge to the worldwide Christian mission today is whether we are willing to pay the cost of following in the footsteps of our incarnate Lord in order to contextualize the gospel. Our failure of communication is a failure of contextualization.

The problem facing every cross-cultural messenger of the gospel can be simply stated. It is this: "How can I, who was born and brought up in one culture, take truth out of the Bible which was addressed to people in a second culture, and communicate it to people who belong to a third culture, without either falsifying the message or rendering it unintelligible? It is this interaction between three cultures which constitute the exciting challenge of cross-cultural communication. And then, when the message has been understood and received by the hearers, further questions arise. How should they relate to their own culture in their conversion, in their ethical lifestyle, and in their church life?[187]

Stott's commitment to and understanding of these challenges enabled him to encourage and support attempts to communicate the gospel in innovative ways and liberated him from conformity to his own cultural upbringing. I experienced this when attempting to reach students and passers-by in the swinging Beatlemania of the 1960's by initiating folk worship in St. Peter's Church, Vere Street, near Oxford Street in London, using guitarists and singers before they became accepted in contemporary services.

12

Discipleship

What does it mean to follow Christ, to be his disciple? Jesus spent three years teaching his disciples what it meant to follow him. John Stott spent his lifetime teaching about discipleship. A disciple is a learner, and there is much to learn about being a Christian. The first books Stott wrote were *Your Confirmation* (1958), which was republished as *Christian Basics: A Handbook of Beginnings, Beliefs and Behavior* (1991), and *Basic Christianity* (1958). They were designed to introduce people to Christianity, to help people know what it means to follow Christ, to be a disciple of Christ.

He began by defining the essence of being a Christian and how to become one. Christianity is not just an intellectual system, a theology or a philosophy, or a creed or a moral code or belonging to a church by undergoing baptism or participating in worship or Holy Communion. The core of Christianity is Christ. A Christian is someone who is personally and decisively committed to Jesus Christ as Savior and Lord. Disciples resolutely turn from their sins in repentance. They have trusted in the Lord Jesus as the One who loved them and gave himself for them on the cross. They have surrendered their life to him, promising to serve and obey him in the fellowship of his church.

Stott authored a formula of four steps to becoming a Christian – an A, B, C, and D:

Admit your sin and need for a Savior.

Believe that Jesus Christ is the Son of God who died on the Cross to be the Savior of the world.

Consider the cost of following Jesus as his disciple.

Do something about it by asking Him into your life as your personal Savior and Lord (Rev. 3:20).[188]

What was unique about this formula was Stott's emphasis on considering the *cost* of following Jesus as his disciple, as Jesus himself also emphasized (Luke 14:25–35). To follow Christ is to renounce all lesser loyalties. Salvation is not offered for nothing. There is no cheap grace.

First, there must be a renunciation of sin. This, in a word, is repentance. ... Repentance is a definite turn from every thought, word, deed and habit which is known to be wrong.

Secondly, there must be a renunciation of self. In order to follow Christ we must not only forsake isolated sins, but renounce the very principle of self-will which lies at the root of all acts of sin. To follow Christ is to surrender to him the rights over our own lives. ... It is to deny ourselves and to take up the cross (Matt. 8:34–38). It is to lose our life. ... The man who commits himself to Christ, therefore, loses himself, not by the absorption of his personality in Christ's personality but by the submission of his will to Christ's will. ... The astonishing idea is current in some circles today that we can enjoy the benefits of Christ's salvation without accepting the challenge of his sovereign lordship. Such an unbalanced notion is not to be found in the New Testament. ... To make Christ Lord is to bring every department of our public and private lives under his control: career, marriage, home, money, time.

     ... If, then, you suffer from moral anaemia, take my advice and steer clear of Christianity. If you want to live a life of easy-going self-indulgence, whatever you do, do not become a Christian. But if you want a life of self-discovery, deeply satisfying to the nature God has given you; if you want a life of adventure in which you have the privilege of serving him and your fellow men; if you want a life in which to express something of the overwhelming gratitude you are beginning to feel for him who died for you, then I urge you to yield your life without reserve and without delay, to your Lord and Savior, Jesus Christ.[189]

Stott made a point of it that each person has to decide for him or herself and make a personal commitment to follow Christ. He highlighted Revelation 3:20, "Behold, I stand at the door and knock. If anyone hears my voice and opens the door, I will come in and eat with that person, and they with me." In 1853 the British artist Holman Hunt painted a picture of this verse. He called it *The Light of the World*. The art critic John Ruskin described the work: "On the left-hand side of the picture is seen the door of the human soul. It is fast-barred; its bars and nails are rusty; it is knitted and bound to its stanchions by creeping tendrils of ivy, showing that it has never been opened. A bat hovers about it; its threshold is overgrown with brambles, nettles and fruitless corn. ... Christ approaches it in the night-time."[190] Stott comments:

First, who lives in the house? The house is representative of every human heart and life, and the occupant is the individual you or I.

Secondly, who is the visitor? It is the historic Jesus.

Thirdly, what is he doing? He is standing at our door knocking and speaking. He stands patiently; he knocks gently; he speaks softly. He forces an entry into nobody's life.

Fourthly, what does he want to do? He wants to come in as Savior and Lord. We must surrender absolutely and unconditionally to the lordship of Jesus Christ.

Fifthly, what must we do? We must hear his voice. Next, we must open the door. To open the door to Jesus Christ is a pictorial way of describing an act of faith in him as our Savior and an act of submission to him as our Lord. You can believe in Christ intellectually and admire him; you can say your prayers to him through the keyhole (I did for many years); you can push coins at him under the door; you can be moral, decent, upright and good; you can be religious and pious; you can have been baptized and confirmed; you can be deeply versed in the philosophy of religion; you can be a theological student and even an ordained minister – and still have not opened the door to Christ. There is no substitute for this.[191]

He went on to describe his own personal experience. On 13 February 1938, about 10:00 p.m., he confessed his sins, thanked Christ for dying for him, and asked him to come into his life. He wrote in his diary the next day: "Up to now Christ has been on the circumference and I have but asked him to guide me instead of giving him complete control. Behold! He stands at the door and knocks. I have heard him and now is he come into my house. He has cleansed it and now rules therein."[192]

The process of learning to be a disciple that follows commitment to Christ is called "sanctification." It is growing as a Christian after being born again into a new life in Christ.

Sanctification describes the process by which justified Christians are changed into the likeness of Christ. When God justifies us, he *declares* us righteous through Christ's death for us; when he sanctifies us, he *makes* us righteous through the power of his Holy Spirit within us. Justification concerns our outward status of acceptance with God; sanctification concerns our inward growth in holiness of character. Further, whereas our justification is sudden and complete, so that we shall never be more justified than we were on the day of our conversion, our sanctification is gradual and incomplete. New birth is a sudden and almost instantaneous crisis. The dramatic crisis of birth is followed by the laborious process of growth. [*Christian Basics* by John Stott. Copyright ©1991 John R.W. Stott. Reproduced by permission of Hodder & Stoughton][193]

Stott then points to four main areas of Christian growth, which I summarize here:[194]

First, *we are to grow in faith*. Faith is trust in Jesus Christ as Savior. Faith is reasonable, though it can go beyond the limits of reason. It is not irrational. There are degrees of faith. "As we read the Bible, meditate on the absolute reliability of God's character, and put his promises to a test, our faith will ripen"[195] (2 Thess. 1:3).

Secondly, *we are to grow in love*. Neither Christians nor churches are always conspicuous for the quality of their loving. "We urge you, brothers, to love one another more and more" (1 Thess. 4:10). Paul also prayed that their love would "increase and overflow" (1 Thess. 3:12).

Thirdly, *we are to grow in knowledge*. "Christianity lays great emphasis on the importance of knowledge, rebukes anti-intellectualism for the negative, paralyzing thing it is, and traces many of our problems to our ignorance."[196] "In your thinking be adults" (1 Cor. 14:20). The Hebrew concept of knowing was never purely intellectual. It went beyond "understanding" to "experiencing." Knowing God in Jesus Christ, which is the essence of being a Christian, means a living, personal relationship to him (Phil 3:8,10; Col. 1:10; 2 Pet. 3:18).

Fourthly, *we are to grow in holiness*. "And we all, who with unveiled faces reflect the Lord's glory, are being transformed into his likeness with ever-increasing glory, which comes from the Lord, who is the Spirit" (2 Cor. 3:18).

1. Holiness is Christlikeness, and sanctification is the process of being transformed into his image.

2. Sanctification is a gradual process: "are being transformed."

3. Holiness is the work of the Holy Spirit. The secret of sanctification is not that we struggle to live like Christ, but that Christ comes by his Spirit to live in us.

4. Our part is to contemplate and so reflect the glory of the Lord. Our contemplation will mean seeking him in the Scriptures in order to worship him.

"The carpenter of Nazareth is still busy with his tools. Now by the chisel of pain, now by the hammer of affliction, now by the plane of adverse circumstance, as well as through experiences of joy, he is shaping us into an instrument of righteousness."[197] Stott responds with a traditional prayer:

O Jesus, Master-Carpenter of Nazareth,
who on the cross through wood and nails has wrought man's full salvation,
wield well your tools in this your workshop, that we who come to you rough-hewn,
may be fashioned into a truer beauty and a greater usefulness, by your hand,
who with the Father and the Holy Spirit lives and reigns, one God,
world without end.

Discipleship requires discipline. "Watch the discipline of your Christian life. Be diligent in daily prayer and Bible-reading, in church-going and attendance at the Lord's Supper. Read helpful books. Seek out Christian friends. Get busy in some form of service. Yield yourself without reserve each day to the power of the Holy Spirit who is within you. Then step by step you will advance along the road of holiness and grow towards full spiritual maturity."[198]

Stott was notorious for his early rising and morning devotions – his quiet time reading the Scriptures and prayer. He read through the Bible every year and was faithful in his prayer life. He also wrote about the importance of prayer.

> Men and women are at their noblest and best when they are on their knees before God in prayer. To pray is not only to be truly godly; it is also to be truly human. For here are human beings, made by God like God and for God, spending time in fellowship with God. So prayer is an authentic activity in itself, irrespective of any benefits it may bring to us. Yet it is also one of the most effective of all the means of grace. I doubt if anybody has ever become at all Christlike who has not been diligent in prayer. There are at least five different kinds of prayers, all of which should find a place in our private devotions.
>
> 1. *The look up to God.* This is worship. It is to seek to give to God the glory which is due his name (Ps. 105:3). Worship is the best of all antidotes to our own self-centeredness, the most effective way to "disinfect us of egotism" (W.E. Sangster). In true worship we turn the searchlight of our mind and heart upon God and temporarily forget about our troublesome and usually intrusive selves.
>
> 2. *The look in at ourselves.* This leads to confession. It is a healthy discipline to review our day and call to mind our failures. Not to do so tends to make us slapdash about sin and encourages us to presume upon God's mercy, whereas to make a habit of doing so humbles us and shames us and increases our longing for greater holiness.
>
> 3. *The look around at others.* This is intercession. We (like Jesus and Paul) should include other people in our prayers; it may be the best service we

can render them. The more specific and concrete we can be in our prayers, the better.

4. *The look back to the past.* This should lead to thanksgiving (Ps. 103:2). At the close of each day it seems right to look back over it in order to recall not only our sins but also God's mercies.

5. *The look to the future.* This is petition or supplication. But God knows our needs; we do not need to tell him. And in his love he wants to supply them; we do not need to bully or badger him. So why pray? What is the point? John Calvin gave a thorough answer to these questions. He wrote: "Believers do not pray with a view of informing God about things unknown to him, or of exciting him to do his duty, or of urging him as though he were reluctant. On the contrary, they pray in order that they may arouse themselves to seek him, that they may exercise their faith in meditating on his promises, that they may relieve themselves from their anxieties, by pouring them into his bosom; in a word, that they may declare that from him alone they hope and expect, both for themselves and for others, all good things." The purpose of petitionary prayer, then, is neither to inform God as though he were ignorant, nor to persuade him as though he were reluctant. It is not to bend God's will to ours, but rather to align our will to his. [*Christian Basics* by John Stott. Copyright ©1991 John R.W. Stott. Reproduced by permission of Hodder & Stoughton][199]

Aligning our will to God's will requires renunciation of sin and self-centeredness. Stott calls this the first great secret of holiness. Jesus said, "If any man would come after me, let him deny himself and take up his cross and follow me" (Mark 8:34). This is Jesus's figure of speech for self-denial. Every disciple of Jesus is to "behave like a condemned criminal and carry his cross to the place of execution."[200] Paul uses this metaphor in Galatians: "Those who belong to Christ Jesus have crucified the flesh with its passions and desires" (Gal. 5:24). "We must not only take up our cross and walk with it, but actually see that the execution takes place. We are actually to take the flesh, our willful and wayward self, and (metaphorically speaking) nail it to the cross. This is Paul's graphic description of repentance, of turning our back on the old life of selfishness and sin, repudiating it finally and utterly."[201]

What does this mean?

The old nature, our willful and wayward self, our former life without Christ, what Paul calls "the flesh," is to be mortified or crucified. Stott expanded on this thought.

First, a Christian's rejection of his old nature is to be *pitiless.* Crucifixion in the Graeco-Roman world was not a pleasant form of execution, nor was it administered to nice or refined people; it was reserved for the worst criminals, which is why it was such a shameful thing for Jesus Christ to be crucified. If, therefore, we are to "crucify" our flesh, it is plain that the flesh is not something respectable to be treated with courtesy and deference, but something so evil that it deserves no better fate than to be crucified.

Secondly, our rejection of the old nature will be *painful*. Crucifixion was a form of execution "attended with intense pain." And which of us does not know the acute pain of inner conflict when "the fleeting pleasures of sin" are renounced?

Thirdly, the rejection of our old nature is to be *decisive*. Although death by crucifixion was a lingering death, it was a certain death. Criminals who were nailed to a cross did not survive. John Brown draws out the significance of this fact for us: "Crucifixion ... produced death not suddenly but gradually. ... True Christians ... do not succeed in completely destroying it (that is, the flesh) while here below; but they have fixed it to the cross, and they are determined to keep it there till it expire." When we came to Jesus Christ, we repented. We "crucified" everything we knew to be wrong. We took our old self-centered nature, with all its sinful passions and desires, and nailed it to the cross. And this repentance of ours was decisive, as decisive as a crucifixion. So, Paul says, if we crucified the flesh, we must leave it there to die. We must renew every day this attitude towards sin of ruthless and uncompromising rejection.

So widely is this biblical teaching neglected, that it needs to be further enforced. The first great secret of holiness lies in the degree and the decisiveness of our repentance. If besetting sins persistently plague us, it is either because we have never truly repented, or because, having repented, we have not maintained our repentance. It is as if, having nailed our old nature to the cross, we keep wistfully returning to the scene of its execution. We begin to fondle it, to caress it, to long for its release, even to try to take it down again from the cross. We need to learn to leave it there. When some jealous, or proud, or malicious or impure thought invades our mind we must kick it out at once. It is fatal to begin to examine it and consider whether we are going to give in or not. We have declared war on it; we are not going to resume negotiations. We have settled the issue for good; we are not going to reopen it. We have crucified the flesh; we are never going to draw the nails.[202]

The other side of the secret of holiness is to walk by the Spirit, to be led by the Spirit. "Whoever sows to please their flesh, from the flesh will reap destruction; whoever sows to please the Spirit, from the Spirit will reap eternal life" (Gal. 6:8). The Christian's life is likened to a farm; and the flesh and the

Spirit are two fields in which we may grow seed. The harvest we reap depends on where and what we sow.

> This is a vitally important and much neglected principle of holiness. We are not the helpless victims of our nature, temperament, and environment. On the contrary, what we become depends largely on how we behave; our character is shaped by our conduct. According to Galatians 5 the Christian's duty is to "walk by the Spirit," according to Galatians 6 to "sow to the Spirit." Thus, the Holy Spirit is likened both to the path along which we walk (Gal. 5) and to the field in which we sow (Gal. 6). How can we expect to reap the fruit of the Spirit if we do not sow in the field of the Spirit? The old adage is true: "Sow a thought, reap an act; sow an act, reap a habit; sow a habit, reap a character; sow a character, reap a destiny." This is good biblical teaching. ...
>
> To "sow to the flesh" is to pander to it, to cosset, cuddle and stroke it, instead of crucifying it. The seeds we sow are largely thoughts and deeds. Every time we allow our mind to harbor a grudge, nurse a grievance, entertain an impure fantasy, or wallow in self-pity, we are sowing to the flesh. Every time we linger in bad company whose insidious influence we know we cannot resist, every time we lie in bed when we ought to be up and praying, every time we read [view] pornographic literature, every time we take a risk which strains our self-control, we are sowing, sowing, sowing to the flesh. Some Christians sow to the flesh every day and wonder why they do not reap holiness. Holiness is a harvest; whether we reap it or not depends almost entirely on what and where we sow.
>
> To "sow to the Spirit" is the same as "to set the mind on the Spirit" (Rom. 6:8) and to "walk by the Spirit" (Gal. 5:16,25). Again, the seeds we sow are our thoughts and deeds. ... By the books we read, the company we keep and the leisure occupations we pursue we can be "sowing to the Spirit." ...
>
> Therefore, if we want to reap a harvest of holiness, our duty is twofold. First we must avoid sowing to the flesh, and secondly we must keep sowing to the Spirit. We must ruthlessly eliminate the first and concentrate our time and energies on the second. It is another way of saying (as in Gal. 5) that we must "crucify the flesh" and "walk by the Spirit." There is no other way of growing in holiness.[203]

How is it possible to become holy?

Stott's answer is: *Jesus Christ through his Spirit.* One of the greatest works of the Holy Spirit is to conform us to the image of Christ, to form Christ in us (Gal. 4:19), to bring forth in our lives his fruit of Christlikeness.[204]

How do we keep sowing to the Spirit in everyday life?

By following the example of Jesus and obeying his commands. Stott expounded it in his Bible studies on the Upper Room Discourse at Urbana 1970. In principle Jesus taught by example: in the footwashing and in his commandment, "Now that I, your Lord and Teacher, have washed your feet, you also should wash one another's feet. I have set you an example that you should do as I have done for you" (John 13:14,15). Jesus calls us to serve others.

> Think of some of the needy people we tend to neglect. Is Christ calling us to some hidden backroom job "serving tables," when we would rather be in the limelight of publicity? Is he calling us to spend time with somebody who is lonely or emotionally unstable or mentally sick, when we would rather relax with our friends? Or to give ourselves in genuine friendship – not superficial but sacrificial – to someone hooked on drugs, and stand by him faithfully during the painful period of withdrawal? Is he calling us to work with penitence and without paternalism in a rundown inner-city area or ghetto? Are we meant to offer our lives in Christ's service in a developing country abroad – as a doctor, nurse, teacher, agriculturalist or social worker – when it would be more lucrative and more respectable to pursue our profession at home? Or should we stay at home and get involved with people in the secular community – perhaps with hippies [dropouts], whom Ted Schroder (one of my colleagues in London) has described as "the largest unreached tribe in the world today." He has added, "We don't learn their language, we don't study their culture, and we don't live among them." It is in such ways as these that we are to follow the example of Jesus our Teacher and Lord today, washing people's feet, sacrificing ourselves to serve them. As he girded himself with a towel, we are (in Peter's expressive phrase), to clothe ourselves with humility (1 Pet. 5:5). I do not think it would be an exaggeration to say that if there is no humble service in our lives, nothing comparable to Christ's washing of the apostles' feet, we can hardly qualify as the disciples of Jesus. For a disciple is not above his teacher, nor a servant above his lord.[205]

In his exposition of John 15, Stott focused on the threefold duty of the Christian. This is Jesus Christ's own portrait of a balanced Christian disciple. It concerns three major relationships – to the Lord, to the church, and to the world.

1. *The Christian and the Lord* (John 15:1–11). Abide in Christ as the branch in the vine and bear much fruit. The fruitfulness is righteous conduct, the moral qualities of justice, self-control, fair dealing, and compassion toward the needy (Isa. 5:8–23). Fruitfulness means Christlikeness – the fruit of the Spirit. The secret of Christian fruitfulness is pruning. Pain, suffering, sorrow, sickness, loss, bereavement, disappointment, and frustrated

ambition are all part of the pruning activity of God the gardener. Not that this is a complete explanation of the meaning of suffering. But it is a partial explanation (Heb. 12:10). As Malcolm Muggeridge said, "Supposing you eliminated suffering, what a dreadful place the world would be! I would almost rather eliminate happiness. The world would be the most ghastly place because everything that corrects the tendency of this unspeakable little creature, man, to feel over-important and over-pleased with himself will disappear. He's bad enough now but he would be absolutely intolerable if he never suffered."[206]

Some form of suffering is virtually indispensable to holiness (1 Pet. 4:1). What does it mean to abide in Christ? The New Testament description of a Christian is that he is "in Christ," and to be "in Christ" means to be united to him. To "abide" in Christ is to develop this already existing relationship. J.C. Ryle paraphrased our Lord's command: "Abide in me. Cling to me. Stick fast to me. Live the life of close and intimate communion with me. Get nearer and nearer to me. Roll every burden on me. Cast your whole weight on me. Never let go your hold on me for a moment."[207]

2. *The Christian and the church* (John 15:12–17). Love one another. The chief characteristic of church members should be mutual love. We must set our love upon one another in prayer and in practical service, seeking each other's good actively, for this is the meaning of love.

3. *The Christian and the world* (John 15:18–25). The world is what we call secular society, a community that rejects or ignores Christ, and of which Satan is both prince and god. The world's attitude to the church is hostility and antagonism. The cause of the world's hostility is their ignorance of God. Dietrich Bonhoeffer in *The Cost of Discipleship* wrote, "Discipleship means allegiance to the suffering Christ, and it is not at all surprising that Christians should be called upon to suffer."[208]

How are we to react to this hostile, hating, persecuting world?

We are to witness to the world of Christ. The Holy Spirit will bear witness through the church. Stott quotes Malcolm Muggeridge again: "Sometimes on foolish television and radio panels, someone asks me what I most want, what I should most like to do in the little that remains of my life, and I nowadays truthfully answer, and it is truthful, 'I should like my light to shine, even if only very fitfully, like a match struck in a dark cavernous night and then flickering out.'"[209]

In his exposition of Ephesians 4:17–5:4, Stott's theme is the integration of Christian experience (what we are), Christian theology (what we believe), and Christian ethics (how we behave). He emphasized that being, thought, and action belong together and must never be separated.

For what we are governs how we think, and how we think determines how we act. We are God's new society, a people who have put off the old life and put on the new; that is what he has made us. … We must actively cultivate a Christian life. For holiness is not a condition into which we drift. We are not passive spectators of a sanctification God works in us. On the contrary, we have purposefully to "put away" from us all conduct that is incompatible with our new life in Christ, and to "put on" a lifestyle compatible with it. … Let no one say that doctrine does not matter! Good conduct arises out of good doctrine. It is only when we have grasped clearly who we are in Christ, that the desire will grow within us to live a life that is worthy of our calling and fitting to our character as God's new society.[210]

Stott applies this to sexuality, speech, emotions, anger, and relationships in marriage, family, and the work place. None of this is easy, for we have a great enemy in the devil, his wiles and the principalities and powers that are arrayed against us. To stand against the devil we need the whole armor of God (Eph. 6:10–20). We are engaged in a spiritual war with the hosts of wickedness that seek to defeat and control us. Therefore, we have to be vigilant about our sanctification. Christlikeness is not automatic but requires application on our part.

In the Sermon on the Mount the values and standards of Jesus are in direct conflict with the commonly accepted values and standards of the world.

The beatitudes paint a comprehensive portrait of the Christian disciple. We see him first alone on his knees before God, acknowledging his spiritual poverty and mourning over it. This makes him meek or gentle in all his relationships, since honesty compels him to allow others to think of him what before God he confesses himself to be. Yet he is far from acquiescing in his sinfulness, for he hungers and thirsts after righteousness, longing to grow in grace and goodness.

We see him next with others, out in the human community. His relationship with God does not cause him to withdraw from society, nor is he insulated from the world's pain. On the contrary, he is in the thick of it, showing mercy to those battered by adversity and sin. He is transparently sincere in all his dealings and seeks to play a constructive role as a peacemaker. Yet he is not thanked for his efforts, but rather opposed, slandered, insulted and persecuted on account of the righteousness for which he stands and the Christ with whom he is identified.

Surely a man or woman is "blessed", that is, who has the approval of God and finds self-fulfillment as a human being.[211]

Stott gave major emphasis to the *salt* and *light* metaphors Jesus applied to Christians; he continually used salt and light to describe the role of the Christian disciple in society. He concluded his study of the Sermon on the Mount with the absolute necessity of understanding the radical choice before the follower of Jesus: the choice of life itself. One way leads to life, the other to destruction; one is a narrow road, the other is broad; we build our lives either on the rock or on the sand.

> Jesus does not set before his followers a string of easy ethical rules, so much as a set of values and ideals which is entirely distinctive from the way of the world. He summons us to renounce the prevailing secular culture in favor of the Christian counter-culture. Repeatedly during our study we have heard his call to his people to be different from everybody else. The first time this became clear was in his commission to us to be both "the salt of the earth" and "the light of the world". For these metaphors set the Christian and non-Christian communities over against each other as recognizably, indeed, fundamentally, distinct. The world is like rotting food, full of the bacteria which causes its disintegration; Jesus' followers are to be its salt, arresting its decay. The world is a dark and dismal place, lacking sunshine, living in shadow; Jesus' followers are to be its light, dispelling its darkness and its gloom.
>
> From then on the opposing standards are graphically described, and the way of Jesus commended. Our righteousness is to be deeper because it reaches even our hearts, and our love broader because it embraces even our enemies. In piety we are to avoid the ostentation of hypocrites and in prayer the verbosity of pagans. Instead our giving, praying and fasting are to be real with no compromise of our Christian integrity. For our treasure we are to choose what endures through eternity, not what disintegrates on earth, and for our master God, not money or possessions. As for our ambition (what preoccupies our mind) this must not be our own material security, but the spread of God's rule and righteousness in the world. ... Here then is the alternative, either to follow the crowd or to follow our Father in heaven, either to be a reed swayed by the winds of public opinion or to be ruled by God's Word, the revelation of his character and will. And the overriding purpose of the Sermon on the Mount is to present us with this alternative, and so to face us with the indispensable necessity of choice.[212]

Nowhere is the necessity of choice more apparent than in the disparity between the rich and the poor, between those who live in affluent communities and those who exist in poverty without the amenities of a prosperous society. Stott addressed this in his commentary on Section 9 of the Lausanne Covenant, which stated: "All of us are shocked by the poverty of millions and disturbed by the injustices which cause it. Those of us who live in affluent circumstances accept our duty to develop a simple lifestyle in order to contribute more generously to both relief and evangelism."[213]

> Those of us who live in comfort have a duty to develop a simple lifestyle. What does it mean for the affluent to develop a simple style of living? Some wished that the adjective were a comparative and read "a simpler lifestyle". [This was the opinion of Ruth Graham who compared the life of a bachelor, like Stott, with a mother, like her, with children who needed her to provide them with more than just the minimum according to their potential needs.] But even this would pose problems for us: how much simpler? And in any case, simpler than what? "Poverty", "simplicity" and "generosity" are all relative and are bound to mean different things to different people. ... Scripture lays down no absolute standards. It does not encourage an austere and negative asceticism, nor does it forbid the possession of private property (Acts 5:4); and it commands us to enjoy with gratitude the good gifts of our Creator (e.g. 1 Tim. 4:1–5; 6:17). But it implies that some measure of equality is more pleasing to God than disparity, and its appeal to believers to be generous is based on the grace of our Lord Jesus Christ, because grace means generosity (1 Cor. 8:8–15). Every Christian should be content with the necessities of life (1 Tim. 6:6–8), but every Christian must make his own conscientious decision before God where he draws the line between necessities and luxuries.[214]

Stott himself strove to live simply and was generous towards others with gifts and the allocation of the royalties of his books to fund the education of pastors in the Majority World. He felt keenly the privileges he enjoyed: his childhood, his education, his position as the Rector of a prestigious church, his accommodation in a rectory in the wealthy West End of London, the support of his staff and friends, his coastal retreat in Wales, and opportunities to travel throughout the world. As a chaplain to the Queen he occasionally enjoyed the hospitality of the Royal family but he never forgot that he was a servant of the King of kings and Lord of lords. He sacrificed material advantages for the sake of the gospel. He was a radical disciple of Christ and chose that designation as the title of his last book.[215]

In his teaching and writing he never considered that there were first-class and second-class Christian disciples. All Christian believers were called to be disciples of Christ. He believed in the priesthood of all believers. All Christians were called to be ministers of the gospel. He incorporated every-member ministry in his leadership of the church. His 1968 book *One People* emphasized the necessity for the training and commissioning of lay people for Christian service. He founded the London Institute for Contemporary Christianity to provide resources for those who would not be able to attend theological colleges and seminaries. He applied the teachings of Jesus to every part of life, including work in the secular world where Christian disciples could witness and serve more effectively than was possible for clergy. His frequent use of the salt and light metaphors Jesus taught, highlighted his concern that *all* Christians should penetrate and illuminate the world as missionaries of the gospel. He echoed the encouragement of Peter, that all followers of Christ are commissioned to be "a chosen people, a royal priesthood, a holy nation, a people belonging to God, that you may declare the praises of him who called you out of darkness into his marvelous light" (1 Pet. 2:9).

13

The Kingdom of God

In his 1954 book, *Men with a Message*, which was republished in 1964 as *Basic Introduction to the New Testament*, Stott summarized Jesus' theology of the kingdom of God.[216] I summarize that teaching.

When Jesus began his ministry his first recorded words were: "The time has come. ... The kingdom of God has come near. Repent and believe the good news!" (Mark 1:15). His message concerned the character and the coming of the kingdom of God. His dominant theme concerned the kingdom: what it was, how to enter it, and how to live worthily as its citizen. "I must proclaim the good news of the kingdom of God to the other towns also, because that is why I was sent" (Luke 4:43).

The Old Testament attests to the ultimate sovereignty of God. God is the king of all the nations, but he is above all, King of Israel. The prophets looked forward to the day when God would establish his own kingdom on earth. This Messianic kingdom had four characteristics:

First, it would be *just*.

Secondly, the Messiah's reign would usher in *peace*.

The third characteristic would be *stability*.

Fourthly, the Messianic kingdom would be *universal*. "His rule will extend from sea to sea, and from the River to the ends of the earth" (Zech. 9:10). These four characteristics of the future, ideal kingdom are combined in Isaiah 9:6–7.

In comparing the fulfilment with the expectation, how does the kingdom of God, as Jesus announced it, exhibit the characteristics so clearly foretold and when did it or will it come?

The character of God's kingdom was widely different from the Messianic kingdom commonly envisaged. Its blessings were to be spiritual rather than material, and its glory was only to be revealed through suffering. There was great misunderstanding of this, which caused Jesus to conceal it from the public. This has become known as the famous "Messianic secret" (Matt. 13:11).

This kingdom of God in the teaching of Jesus is a spiritual conquest of men and women. Its sphere is of this world but its origin is divine; its character is the spread of the truth by which people are to be set free (John 18:37; 8:32,36). It is not imperialistic; it has no territorial rights or ambitions. It works like leaven, conquering not by force from without but by grace from within (Matt. 13:33).

In the story of the rich young ruler Jesus equated inheriting eternal life with entering the kingdom of God. To be saved and to be a citizen of the kingdom of God are one and the same thing. The four characteristics of the Messianic kingdom commonly envisaged were fulfilled in the kingdom of God as announced by Jesus, albeit with a significant alteration of emphasis.

First, *righteousness*. Moral repentance is the first condition of entry into the kingdom, involving not just the profession of the lips but the obedience of the life (Matt. 7:21). It is to be sought with hunger and thirst (Matt. 5:6; 6:33), as a gift of God's grace rather than as an achievement of human effort (Luke 18:14).

Secondly, *peace*. It is freedom from anxiety, for faith banishes fear (Matt. 6:25–34; Luke 12:22–31). Peaceful civil relationships find their fulfilment in the harmony of the Christian community.

Thirdly, *stability*, which would come through the everlasting reign of God in the hearts of his subjects. It is a kingdom that would come in lowliness, grow in extent across the years, and be consummated at the end of the ages.

Fourthly, *universality*, which would see all races eligible to enter and, indeed, exclude many of those who thought they were the chosen race. The church was to go and make disciples of all nations and be witnesses of the kingdom to the uttermost parts of the earth.

Some think that the kingdom of God has already arrived. This is the school of "realized eschatology." Others think that it is to come in the next age. But the kingdom was coming all the time; and it is still growing. Its progress is twofold: God gives it; and it is received by faith. It comes by grace and faith; by offer and reception; as God gives it and as people receive it.

In the mind of Jesus and the evangelists the kingdom began to come at Christ's baptism. He implied the possibility of entering it then and there. His mighty works of healing were signs of the kingdom. The second manifestation of the kingdom was the transfiguration. The third took place on the cross. The covenant-kingdom with its offer of forgiveness could only be ratified by Christ's blood; only when the King was enthroned on his cross can all men flock into his kingdom. The kingdom also came at the resurrection and at the exaltation. During the forty days that elapsed between Christ's resurrection and ascension he spoke concerning the kingdom of God (Acts 1:3). Pentecost was a further manifestation of the kingdom's coming. So also was the destruction of Jerusalem by the Roman legions under the command of Emperor Titus in A.D. 70. The King rose up in judgment upon his miscreant citizens (Matt. 21:40–43; 22:5–7). Once established, the kingdom's two aspects of grace and judgment were revealed at Pentecost and at the destruction of Jerusalem, both of which will be consummated at the end of the age. All of these events foreshadow, and will be completed at, the final coming of Christ.

Disciples are still to pray "Your kingdom come." The present sowing and growth await the final harvest. That day will be heralded by signs, but its appearing will eventually be sudden and unexpected. It will be a day of separation: "One will be taken and the other left" (Matt. 24:40f.; Luke 17:31–35). The King will sit on his throne of glory and separate the nations as a shepherd separates the sheep from the goats (Matt. 25:31–46). Then will come the final dénouement, and the kingdom will be inherited by those for whom it has been prepared since the creation of the world (v.34). The kingdom will have been consummated.

Jesus clearly taught that the extension of the kingdom is dependent on the response that men and women make to its moral demands. What, then, are the conditions of entry into the kingdom? You must be born from above (John 3:3). It is a deep, inward, revolutionary change of heart effected by the Holy Spirit. But how can this change come about? It is by repentance and faith. People are to believe in Jesus. They are also to surrender their lives. "Whoever wants to be my disciple must deny themselves and take up their cross and follow me" (Mark 8:34). It means renunciation of self. This claim on our total allegiance is one we all need to face squarely today. Jesus never encouraged half-hearted discipleship. He asked for all or nothing. We are to be like a child if we are to enter the kingdom (Matt. 18:3,4).

> God's kingdom is God himself ruling his people, and bestowing upon them all the privileges and responsibilities which his rule implies. To this international God-ruled community, which had replaced the Old Testament national theocracy, Gentiles and Jews belonged on equal terms. Paul is writing while the Roman Empire is at the zenith of its splendor; no signs had yet appeared of its coming decline, let alone of its fall. Yet he sees this other kingdom. Neither Jewish nor Roman but international and interracial, as something more splendid and more enduring than any earthly empire. And he rejoices in its citizenship more even than in his Roman citizenship. Its citizens are free and secure.[217]

Christians have long debated the relationship between the church and the kingdom. They are not identical, for the church is temporal and fallible. The church is the community in which God's kingly rule is revealed, which witnesses to the divine rule and is the first fruits of the redeemed humanity (Jas. 1:18). It lives by new values and standards, and its relationships have been transformed by love. Yet it continues to fail. For it lives in an uneasy tension between the "already" and the "not yet," between the present reality and the future expectation of the kingdom.[218]

The first sign of the kingdom was (and still is) *Jesus himself in the midst of his people* (Luke 17:21; Matt. 18:20), whose presence brings joy, peace and a sense of celebration (John 15:11; 16:33; Mark 2:18–20).

The second sign of the kingdom is *the preaching of the gospel*. The good news points people to the kingdom itself.

The third sign of the kingdom was *exorcism*. Demons are evil, personal intelligences under the command of the devil. Deliverance is only possible in a power encounter in which the name of Jesus is invoked and prevails.

The fourth sign of the kingdom was the *healing and nature miracles* – making the blind see, the deaf hear, the lame walk, the sick whole, raising the dead, stilling the storm, and multiplying loaves and fishes. These are anticipations of the final kingdom from which all disease, hunger, disorder, and death will be forever banished.

A fifth sign of the kingdom is the miracle of *conversion and the new birth*. The spell of idols, whether traditional or modern, and of the spirits has been broken (1 Thess. 1:9).

A sixth sign of the kingdom is *the people of the kingdom*, in whom is manifested that cluster of Christlike qualities Paul called "the fruit of the Spirit." Love issues in good works. Good works are signs of the kingdom.

The seventh sign of the kingdom is *suffering*. It was necessary for the King to suffer in order to enter into his glory. To suffer for the sake of righteousness or for our testimony to Jesus, and to bear such suffering courageously, is a clear sign to all beholders that we have received God's salvation or kingdom (Phil. 1:28,29; cf. 2 Thess. 1:5).

God's rule extends only over those who acknowledge it, who have bowed their knee to Jesus and confessed his lordship (Phil. 2:9–11). They are the ones God "has rescued ... from the dominion of darkness and brought ... into the kingdom of the Son he loves" (Col. 1:13). Apart from them, the whole world is "under the control of the evil one," its "prince" and "god" (1 John 5:19;

John 12:31; 2 Cor. 4:4), for at present "we do not see everything subject to" Jesus (Heb. 2:8).

How can Christ claim universal authority if the whole world still lies in Satan's power?

The answer is that over his redeemed people, Jesus is king *de facto*, while it is only *de jure* that he is presently king over the world, his right being still challenged by the usurper. The radical realism of the Bible recognizes both the defeat of evil and its refusal to concede defeat. The kingdom community must act as salt and light in the world to be effective agents for cultural, social, and political change. It is our urgent responsibility to summon all people in Christ's name to turn and humble themselves like little children in order to enter the kingdom and receive its priceless blessing, the salvation of God (Matt. 18:3).[219]

14

Ethics

In 1978 John Stott preached a series of sermons at All Souls Church on "Issues Facing Britain Today." They grew into lectures at the London Institute for Contemporary Christianity. Subsequently, in 1984, he published *Issues Facing Christians Today: a major appraisal of contemporary social and moral questions*. In his Introduction he wrote a disclaimer.

> I am in no sense a specialist in moral theology or social ethics and I have no particular expertise or experience in some of the fields into which I trespass ... what I am venturing to offer the public is not a polished professional piece but the rough-hewn amateur work of an ordinary Christian who is struggling to think Christianly, that is, to apply the biblical revelation to the pressing issues of the day. ... Some Christians, anxious above all to be faithful to the revelation of God without compromise, ignore the challenges of the modern world and live in the past. Others, anxious to respond to the world around them, trim and twist God's revelation in their search for relevance. I have struggled to avoid both traps.[220]

He began with a survey of the evangelical heritage of social concern in the eighteenth and nineteenth centuries. Then he gave five reasons for the evangelical renunciation of social responsibility in the twentieth century: (1) a reaction against theological liberalism; (2) a reaction against the so-called social gospel that sought to transform humanity into the kingdom of God; (3) the widespread disillusion and pessimism that followed World War I; (4) the spread of premillennialism through the Scofield Bible that saw no point in trying to reform the world; (5) the growth of the middle class and their identification of Christianity with their culture.

Stott went on to lay out the biblical basis for social concern and why Christians should get involved in the issues of the day. There are five great doctrines of the Bible that should be sufficient to convince Christians of their social responsibility.

1. *A fuller doctrine of God*. God is concerned for the whole of mankind and for the whole of human life in all its color and complexity.

First, the living God is the God of nature as well as of religion, of the "secular" as well as of the "sacred." For everything is "sacred" in the sense that it belongs to God, and nothing is "secular" in the sense that God is excluded from it. We should be more grateful than we usually are for the good gifts of a good Creator – for sex, marriage, and the family, for the beauty and wonder of the natural world, for work and leisure, for friendships and the experience of inter-racial inter-cultural community, for music and other kinds of creative art that enrich the quality of human life.

Secondly, the living God is the God of creation as well as of the Covenant. The Bible begins with the nations, not Israel; with Adam not Abraham; with the creation not the covenant. Social compassion and justice mattered in the nations as well as in Israel (see the book of Amos). It is clear from the Old Testament that God hates injustice and oppression everywhere, and that he loves and promotes justice everywhere.

Thirdly, the living God is the God of justice as well as of justification.

2. ***A fuller doctrine of man.*** A human being might be defined from a biblical perspective as "a body-soul-in-community." For that is how God has made us. So, if we truly love our neighbors, and because of their worth desire to serve them, we shall be concerned for their total welfare, the wellbeing of their soul, body, and community. Christians seek in whatever way they can to express their solidarity with the poor and hungry, the deprived and disadvantaged. Why have they done it? Because of the Christian doctrine of man, male and female, all made in the image of God, though also all fallen. Because people matter. Because every man, woman, and child has an intrinsic value as a human being. Once we see this, we shall both set ourselves to liberate people from everything dehumanizing and count it a privilege to serve them, to do everything in our power to make human life more human.

3. ***A fuller doctrine of Christ.*** Incarnational mission, whether evangelistic or social or both, necessitates a costly identification with people in their actual situation. Jesus of Nazareth was moved with compassion by the sight of needy human beings, whether sick or bereaved, hungry, harassed or helpless; should not his people's compassion be aroused by the same sights?

4. ***A fuller doctrine of salvation.***

First, we must not separate salvation from the kingdom of God. For the kingdom of God is God's dynamic rule, breaking into human history through Jesus, confronting, combating and overcoming evil, spreading the wholeness of personal and communal wellbeing, taking possession of his people in total blessing and with total demand.

Secondly, we must not separate Jesus the Savior from Jesus the Lord. The affirmations "Jesus is Lord" and "Jesus is Savior" are almost interchangeable. And his lordship extends far beyond the religious bit of our lives. It embraces the whole of our experience, public and private, home and work, church membership and civic duty, evangelistic and social responsibilities.

Thirdly, we must not separate faith from love. True faith issues in love, and true love issues in service. Saving faith and serving love belong together.

5. *A fuller doctrine of the church.* We need to recover what could be described as the church's "double-identity." On the one hand the church is a "holy" people, called out of the world to belong to God. But on the other it is a "worldly" people, in the sense of being sent back into the world to witness and to serve.

These five doctrines constitute the biblical basis for mission, for both evangelistic and social responsibility. They lay upon us an obligation to be involved in the life of the world. Stott quoted William Temple, who, in his 1942 book *Christianity and Social Order* wrote, "The Church is committed to the everlasting Gospel; it must never commit itself to an ephemeral program of detailed action."[221] Readers of Temple will know that he was very far from saying that religion and politics do not mix. His point was different, namely that "the Church is concerned with principles and not policy."[222] The reasons why he believed the Church as a whole should refrain from "direct political action" by developing and advocating specific programs could be summed up as "integrity" (the church lacks the necessary expertise, though some of her members may have it), "prudence" (because she may prove to be mistaken and so be discredited), and "justice" (because different Christians hold different opinions, and the church should not side with even a majority of its members against an equally loyal minority). How to proceed when problems are complex and divisive? He commends developing a "Christian mind," namely a mind that has firmly grasped the basic presuppositions of Scripture and is thoroughly informed with biblical truth. Harry Blamires popularized this expression in his book by that title. The Christian mind is "a mind trained, informed, equipped to handle data of secular controversy within a framework of reference which is constructed of Christian presuppositions."[223] We should seek to educate the public conscience to know and desire the will of God. The church should be the conscience of the nation. We should reason with people about the benefits of Christian morality, commending God's law to them by rational arguments.

The bulk of *Issues Facing Christians Today* is taken up with a discussion of Global Issues, Social Issues and Sexual Issues. Global Issues included chapters on "The Nuclear Threat," "Our Human Environment," "North–South Economic Inequality," and "Human Rights." Social Issues included chapters on "Work and Unemployment," "Industrial Relations," "The Multi-Racial Dream and Poverty," "Wealth," and "Simplicity." Sexual Issues included chapters on "Women, Men and God," "Marriage and Divorce," "The Abortion Dilemma," and "Homosexual Partnerships." Some of the material is outdated and therefore it was revised and updated with Stott's approval in 1990 and 1999 by Roy McCloughry. Since the subject matter deserves greater attention than is possible in this book I shall leave it to the reader who is interested in these issues to read the relevant chapters in the original. Needless to say, each topic is given the thorough attention that is characteristic of Stott. The most relevant chapters to the 21st century are those dealing with the environment; the multi-racial dream; women, men and God; abortion; and homosexual partnerships.

Stott changed his mind on the status of the fetus in addressing the problem of abortion. In 1972, in an article in *Christianity Today*, he argued that the fetus throughout the gestation period was "a potential human being in the making, but not yet an independent individual."[224] In another article, in 1980, he claimed that from "fusion onwards the fetus is an unborn child."[225] The chapter in *Issues Facing Christians Today* reflects this later position, that the fetus should be treated as a full human being.

The chapter on homosexual partnerships is an extended discussion of the subject that he later exhaustively addressed in his 1994 commentary on Romans in the exposition of 1:26–27.[226] The history of the world confirms that idolatry tends to immorality; a false image of God leads to a false understanding of sex. Illicit sex degrades peoples' humanness; sex in marriage, as God intended, ennobles it. "God gave them over to shameful lusts" (v.26), which Paul specifies as lesbian practices and male homosexual relationships (v.27). Romans 1:26–27 are a crucial text in the contemporary debate about homosexuality. To act "against nature" means to violate the order God has established, whereas to act "according to nature" means to behave "in accordance with the intention of the Creator" (Cranfield).[227] Jesus refers to the creation narrative in Genesis (Matt. 19:4ff). God instituted marriage as a heterosexual union. A homosexual partnership (however loving and committed it may claim to be) is "against nature" and can never be regarded as a legitimate alternative to marriage.

Timothy Dudley-Smith, in his biography of Stott, commented that,

Since its first publication in 1984, *Issues Facing Christians Today* has been the starting point for many groups or individuals wanting to discern a Christian mind on such diverse but pressing contemporary questions. ... On a variety of preachers' bookshelves it remained a standard work of reference. But the changing nature of such issues, and the working out of the biblical ethic in contemporary practice, present a moving target. In 1990, and again in 1999, much revising and updating were needed.

A full-page review in the journal *Third Way* questioned whether what the book offered could really be called "evangelical ethics" at all, suggesting that the author's thinking owed too much to William Temple's exposition of the congruity between Christian and non-Christian moral reason; and noting that there is little sense of the crises of modernity. Nevertheless, to many intelligent Christians and pastors wrestling with the bewildering world around them, the book offered biblical insights applied to modern problems in a way which, over the sixteen years of its life, no other similar work had yet attempted with the same breadth of interest and overriding faithfulness to Scripture.[228]

15

The Last Things

The four last things that are traditionally subjects of the four Sundays in Advent are Death, Judgment, Heaven, and Hell. Stott dealt with each of these subjects in his writings.

> The "last things" (death, the Parousia, the resurrection, the last judgement and the final destinies of heaven or hell), which are together the focus of eschatology, have always fascinated Christian minds. Yet you [David Edwards] are right to reproach Evangelicals for developing at times an unhealthy preoccupation with them. We have tended both to be too literalistic in our interpretations and to forget that New Testament teaching in this area is not given to satisfy our curiosity but rather to stimulate our holiness, service, witness and hope. ... I myself regret that some Evangelical societies and institutions include in their basis of faith, a particular eschatological viewpoint, and so make it a test of orthodoxy. For I believe that both the interpretation of prophecy and the nature of the millennium belong to the *adiaphora*, in which we should accord one another liberty of opinion. [*Essentials: a liberal-evangelical dialogue*. Copyright ©1988 David L. Edwards & John R.W. Stott. Reproduced by permission of Hodder and Stoughton Limited][229]

In his exposition of John 14 at the 1970 Urbana Conference, Stott dealt with death as seen by Jesus in his Upper Room Discourse.[230]

> *"My Father's house has many rooms; if that were not so, would I have told you that I am going there to prepare a place for you?"* (John 14:2). Jesus bids us think of death not as a leap into the dark unknown, but as a journey to a prepared place. It will not be like arriving in a strange town in a foreign land, where you know nobody, nobody is expecting you and you haven't even made a hotel reservation. No. Just as Jesus sent two of his disciples ahead into the city to prepare for him to eat the Passover (Mark 14:12–16), so now he would go ahead to prepare a place for them. In the

familiar and true expression death is "going home" to a place prepared in our Father's house.

"And if I go and prepare a place for you, I will come back and take you to be with me that you also may be where I am." (John 14:3). Here is a second promise of Christ calculated to reassure us. Having gone ahead to prepare a place for us, he does not expect us to travel there on our own. Instead, he promises to come back in person to fetch us. Christ comes to take us to himself. Is it fanciful to suppose that when the dying martyr Stephen said he saw Jesus *standing* at God's right hand, Jesus has in fact risen from his throne in order to fetch or welcome him? Christ is our destination as well as our escort. *He* comes to take us, and he takes us to *himself.*

This is the essential New Testament revelation about the next life for believers, whether the reference is to the final state after the resurrection or to the intermediate state between death and resurrection. Of the intermediate state Paul said he had a "desire to depart and be with Christ, which is better by far" (Phil. 1:23; cf. 2 Cor. 5:8). Of the final state he wrote "so we will be with the Lord forever" (1 Thess. 4:17).

There is no need for us to speculate about the precise nature of heaven. We are assured on the authority of Jesus Christ that it is the house and home of his Father and ours (there are twenty-two references to the Father in this chapter), that this home is a prepared place containing many rooms or resting places, and that he himself will be there. What more do we need to know? To be certain that where he is, there we shall be also should be enough to satisfy our curiosity and allay our fears.

"I am the way and the truth and the life." (John 14:6). It is a beautiful truth that the Lord Jesus Christ, who is himself our heavenly destination, is in addition our forerunner (who has gone ahead to prepare the way), our personal escort (who comes to fetch us), and the way by which we travel there. The sense in which Jesus Christ is "the way" to the Father is suggested by the other two expressions; namely, that he is also "the truth and the life," that is, the truth about God and the very life of God. ... These, then, are the four positive assertions about the second coming of Christ which he gave to the apostles in order to cure their spiritual heart trouble ("Do not let your hearts be troubled"). And the same promises (if we believe them) will calm our fears in the face of death. Already he is preparing a place for us. Already he is the way along which we are traveling. One day (at his appearing or in a secondary sense at our death) he will come to fetch us and he will take us to himself.

It is those believers who thus keep their eyes on Christ as the Forerunner, the Way, the Escort, and the Destination, whose hearts are set free from the fear of death. Of Henry Venn it is reported that when told he was dying, "the prospect made him so jubilant and high-spirited that his doctor said that his joy at dying kept him alive a further fortnight."[231]

The last book of the Bible is the book of Revelation, which can be and has been interpreted in a variety of ways. Stott recognized that it is full of symbolism, numerology, and mythological imagery. He did not hold with the popular interpretations (the "preterist," "futurist," and "historicist") that it contained references to particular historical events, which belong to the past (the first century), the future (the end of the age), and the span of church history in between. He preferred a fourth school of interpretation that avoided historical particularity and preserved the best of all the three other schools. He called it the "successivo-parallelist" view that was expounded by William Hendricksen in his *More Than Conquerors* (1962) and Michael Wilcock in *I Saw Heaven Opened: the message of Revelation* (1975). Wilcock was Stott's Senior Curate in the late sixties and preached a series of sermons in All Souls on this subject.

This view sees Revelation as a series of dramatic visions, each of which recapitulates the story of the "interadventual period" (the whole era stretching between Christ's two comings) and culminates in the End. The essence of its message concerns the age-long conflict between the Lamb and the dragon, the church and the world, Jerusalem the holy city and Babylon the great city (a conflict that has had many historical manifestations and will have yet more), together with the assurance of Christ's victory.[232]

The triumphant refrain of Revelation is "the Lord reigns." Despite the activity of the devil and his minions, the triumph of God over evil is confidently anticipated. There is an invincible faith in the sovereignty of God in eras of persecution. John's vision of the glorified Jesus permeates the book. It is a vision to cheer the faint and encourage the weary, to stimulate the faithfulness of Christians in the present. The visions have no exclusively particular historical reference. They reveal certain abiding, eternal principles governing Christ and his church that are constantly illustrated in history. The historical situation of the church may alter but the spiritual principles remain. Whatever trials may beset the church, she is secure through the sovereignty of Christ. The world will finally be judged by Christ and overthrown. He will be the King of kings in the new heaven and the new earth.

> For its inner life a sinful church needs the vision of Christ residing in it. For its outer conflict a doubtful church needs the vision of Christ reigning over it. For its ultimate destiny a fearful church needs the vision of Christ returning to it. To a sinful church the residing Christ says: "I know ... Repent!" To a doubtful church the reigning Christ says: "I have conquered. ... Believe!" To a fearful church Christ says: "I am coming soon. ... Endure!" This is

Christ's word to the church of all ages. So the Bride responds, as the Spirit does, with words of joyful expectation: "Amen. Come, Lord Jesus" (Rev. 22:17,20).[233]

In his discussion of the nature of the millennium, the thousand-year period mentioned in Revelation 20, which is the subject of much debate among evangelicals and has spawned much speculative literature about a Rapture, and the return of the Jews to the present nation of Israel, Stott expounded the Amillenialist position, which has three main characteristics.

First, Christ is reigning (incidentally not "on earth", the locale of his rule being nowhere mentioned). Secondly, certain people (including witnesses, martyrs and those "given authority to judge") come to life, reign with Christ and serve as "priests" (vv.4,6). Thirdly, the dragon (Satan) is bound and locked up "to keep him from deceiving the nations anymore" (v.3). What strikes us is that in the rest of the New Testament these three activities characterize the present age, that is, the whole interadventual period. First, Jesus Christ is reigning now. Secondly, his people have been raised with him sharing in his reign (e.g. Eph. 2:6; Col. 3:1–3), and are called kings and priests (1 Pet. 2:5–9; Rev. 1:6; 5:10). "This is the first resurrection," [the apostle] John comments, because it refers to our being raised with Christ now, and not to the resurrection of the body, which will take place only at the end of history (v.5). Thirdly, Satan is bound, having been overthrown by Christ at his first coming. He likened Satan to "a strong man, fully armed", and himself to "someone stronger", who overpowers him, binds him and then robs his house (Luke 11:21–22). The New Testament plainly affirms that Jesus has defeated, dethroned and disarmed the devil, with all the principalities and powers (e.g. Col. 2:15; Heb. 2:14). Probably the best way to understand the binding of Satan in Revelation 20 is to note its purpose, which is "to keep him from deceiving the nations". The missionary advance of the church is possible because Satan is kept from deceiving the nations. [*Essentials: a liberal-evangelical dialogue*. Copyright ©1988 David L. Edwards & John R.W. Stott. Reproduced by permission of Hodder and Stoughton Limited][234]

Perhaps the most controversial aspect of Stott's teaching was his treatment of judgment and hell. He deplored the glibness and glee with which some evangelicals spoke about hell. He thought that a sickness of mind or spirit. On the day of judgment, when some will be condemned, there is going to be "weeping and gnashing of teeth" (Matt. 8:12; 22:13; 24:51; 25:30; Luke 13:28). Stott suggested we should begin to weep at the prospect, as Jeremiah did (Jer. 9:1), as Jesus wept over Jerusalem (Luke 19:41–42), as Paul wept over his own people and the Gentiles who did not believe (Acts 20:31).

set free from the fear of death. Of Henry Venn it is reported that when told he was dying, "the prospect made him so jubilant and high-spirited that his doctor said that his joy at dying kept him alive a further fortnight."[231]

The last book of the Bible is the book of Revelation, which can be and has been interpreted in a variety of ways. Stott recognized that it is full of symbolism, numerology, and mythological imagery. He did not hold with the popular interpretations (the "preterist," "futurist," and "historicist") that it contained references to particular historical events, which belong to the past (the first century), the future (the end of the age), and the span of church history in between. He preferred a fourth school of interpretation that avoided historical particularity and preserved the best of all the three other schools. He called it the "successivo-parallelist" view that was expounded by William Hendricksen in his *More Than Conquerors* (1962) and Michael Wilcock in *I Saw Heaven Opened: the message of Revelation* (1975). Wilcock was Stott's Senior Curate in the late sixties and preached a series of sermons in All Souls on this subject.

This view sees Revelation as a series of dramatic visions, each of which recapitulates the story of the "interadventual period" (the whole era stretching between Christ's two comings) and culminates in the End. The essence of its message concerns the age-long conflict between the Lamb and the dragon, the church and the world, Jerusalem the holy city and Babylon the great city (a conflict that has had many historical manifestations and will have yet more), together with the assurance of Christ's victory.[232]

The triumphant refrain of Revelation is "the Lord reigns." Despite the activity of the devil and his minions, the triumph of God over evil is confidently anticipated. There is an invincible faith in the sovereignty of God in eras of persecution. John's vision of the glorified Jesus permeates the book. It is a vision to cheer the faint and encourage the weary, to stimulate the faithfulness of Christians in the present. The visions have no exclusively particular historical reference. They reveal certain abiding, eternal principles governing Christ and his church that are constantly illustrated in history. The historical situation of the church may alter but the spiritual principles remain. Whatever trials may beset the church, she is secure through the sovereignty of Christ. The world will finally be judged by Christ and overthrown. He will be the King of kings in the new heaven and the new earth.

> For its inner life a sinful church needs the vision of Christ residing in it. For its outer conflict a doubtful church needs the vision of Christ reigning over it. For its ultimate destiny a fearful church needs the vision of Christ returning to it. To a sinful church the residing Christ says: "I know ... Repent!" To a doubtful church the reigning Christ says: "I have conquered. ... Believe!" To a fearful church Christ says: "I am coming soon. ... Endure!" This is

Evangelical leaders hold it today. Do I hold it, however? Well, emotional-ly, I find the concept intolerable and do not understand how people can live with it without either cauterizing their feelings or cracking under the strain. ... What does God's word say? We must open our minds to the possibility that Scripture points us in the direction of annihilation, and that "eternal conscious torment" is a tradition which has to yield to the supreme authority of Scripture. There are four arguments.

First, language. The vocabulary of "destruction" (Matt. 10:28). If to kill is to deprive the body of life, hell would seem to be the deprivation of both physical and spiritual life, that is, an extinction of being. Unbelievers are those who are perishing. The impenitent will finally be destroyed.

Secondly, the imagery of fire. The main function of fire is to secure de-struction. ... The most natural way to understand the reality behind the imagery is that ultimately all enmity and resistance to God will be destroyed. So both the language of destruction and the imagery of fire seem to point to annihilation.

Thirdly, the biblical vision of justice. ... I question whether "eternal con-scious torment" is compatible with the biblical revelation of divine justice.

Fourthly, the problem of universalism. The warnings of Jesus is that there will be a judgement which will involve a separation into two opposite but equally eternal destinies. The eternal existence of the impenitent in hell would be hard to reconcile with the promises of God's final victory over evil, or with the apparently universalistic texts which speak of Christ drawing all men to himself and so on. How can God do this while an unspecified number of people still continue in rebellion against him? It would be easier to hold together the awful reality of hell and the universal reign of God if hell means destruction and the impenitent are no more.

I do not dogmatize about the position to which I have come. I hold it tentatively. But I do plead for a frank dialogue among Evangelicals on the basis of Scripture. I also believe that the ultimate annihilation of the wicked should at least be accepted as a legitimate, biblically founded alternative to their eternal conscious torment. [*Essentials: a liberal-evangelical dialogue.* Copyright ©1988 David L. Edwards & John R.W. Stott. Reproduced by permission of Hodder and Stoughton Limited][235]

Stott's good friend, J.I. Packer, and many other evangelicals, disagreed with this interpretation, as he anticipated. However, it must be conceded that his position was tentative and not central to his preaching of the gospel. He preferred to call himself agnostic on the issue because the biblical teaching was not plain enough to warrant dogmatism.[236] He stood by the wording of the Lausanne

Covenant that "Those who reject Christ repudiate the joy of salvation and condemn themselves to eternal separation from God." Also, the Keele Statement: "A persistent and deliberate rejection of Jesus Christ condemns men to hell." They refer only to people who have heard of Christ but have rejected him, consciously, deliberately, persistently. Such people are not just condemned; they condemn themselves. But what about those who have never heard of Christ? He laid out his answer to this perplexing question in terms of what he understood the New Testament to say:

First, ***all human beings, apart from the intervention and mercy of God, are perishing.*** We are all hell-deserving sinners. Without Christ I am "perishing" and deserve to perish. Stott refers to *The Cross of Christ*, where he wrote about the gravity of sin and the majesty of God.[237] He wanted to say to his contemporaries what Anselm said to his, "You have not yet considered the seriousness of sin." The weakness of the liberal is to praise the good they see in others and to ignore their vanity, obstinacy selfishness, envy, impatience, malice, and lack of self-control.

Secondly, ***human beings cannot save themselves by any religious or righteous acts.***

Thirdly, ***Jesus Christ is the only Savior*** (John 14:6; Acts 4:12).

Fourthly, ***what condition has to be fulfilled in order that they may be saved?*** How much knowledge of Jesus do people have to have before they can believe in him? And how much faith do they have to exercise? What about those who have not heard it? They cannot save themselves, and Christ is the only Savior. Is there any way in which God will have mercy on them, through Christ alone, and not through their own merit? Stott lists a variety of speculative answers to these questions.

> 1. John Paul II in his encyclical *Redemptor Hominis* (1979) wrote: "Man – every man without any exception whatever – has been redeemed by Christ, and ... with man – with each man without any exception whatever – Christ is in a way united, even when man is unaware of it."[238] That kind of unconditional universalism, must, however, be firmly rejected by those who look to Scripture for authoritative guidance.

> 2. The sheep and goats passage in Matthew 25. This is not to be interpreted as salvation by works. The "brothers" are his disciples. Their attitude to Jesus' brothers will be made known by whether they welcome or reject them.

> 3. God knows how people would have responded if they had heard the gospel and will save them or judge them accordingly.

4. God gives everyone a vision of Jesus and therefore an opportunity to repent and believe at the moment of their dying. There is no evidence to support this.

5. God will give everybody an opportunity in the next life to respond to Jesus. This remains a guess and lacks biblical warrant.

6. Norman Anderson has suggested that some people who have never heard of Christ may be brought by their sense of sin to cry to God for mercy and find it on the basis of Christ's atoning work. He cites the Old Testament believers who were saved by grace through faith, even though they knew little if anything about the coming Christ.[239]

Speaking now for myself, although I am attracted by Norman Anderson's concept, and although there may be truth in it, I believe the most Christian stance is to remain agnostic on this question. When somebody asked Jesus, "Lord, are only a few people going to be saved?" he refused to answer. ... The fact is that God, alongside the most solemn warnings about our responsibility to respond to the gospel, has not revealed how he will deal with those who have never heard it. ... I cherish the hope that the majority of the human race will be saved. ... the final vision of the redeemed in the book of Revelation is of "a great multitude that no one could count" (Rev. 7:9). As innumerable as the stars in the sky, the dust of the earth and the grains of sand on the seashores of the world. That is the hope I cherish, and that is the vision that inspires me, even while I remain agnostic about how God will bring it to pass. [*Essentials: a liberal-evangelical dialogue*. Copyright ©1988 David L. Edwards & John R.W. Stott. Reproduced by permission of Hodder and Stoughton Limited][240]

Stott's teaching on hell is an example of Charles Simeon's "moderation on contested and doubtful points of theology [which] contributed to his ultimate success" cited by Daniel Wilson in my Introduction earlier in this book. Stott's teaching is a balance between hellfire and damnation preaching on the one hand and insipid universalism on the other. It is an expression of humility and compassion over dogmatic self-righteousness. It exhibits mercy that triumphs over judgment (Jas. 2:13). He takes hell seriously for he takes Christ seriously. There is a temptation for preachers to go too far, to fall into the trap of thinking that their opinions are infallible, their interpretations are holy writ, and their enthusiasm is Spirit-filled. I will never forget saying to John Stott before entering All Souls Church to preach one Sunday: "I am praying for liberty." He replied to his 26-year-old assistant, "And I am praying for restraint!" He was a model of restraint on issues of the last things, where Scripture emphasizes exhortation and warnings rather than timetables and details about destinations, seeking to encourage repentance and a holy life.

16

Orni-Theology

John Stott was a lifelong bird watcher. In his travels throughout the world he always took his binoculars with him to observe the birds. He claimed, in his book, *The Birds Our Teachers*, that he had seen about 2,500 species.[241] I can well remember accompanying him on a bird-watching trip to Port Aransas, Texas to observe the Whooping Cranes, the rarest of cranes and highly endangered, that wintered there in a wildlife refuge. It was a very cold day as we floated on a sightseeing boat to glimpse the species. While we shivered, he was in his element. When we returned to our home in San Antonio, we hosted an evening with him where he gave us a slide show of his trip to the Canadian Arctic to see the Snowy Owl. He presented me with a copy of *Birds of North America*, which I use to identify the different species that visit the bird feeder outside my window. He subtitled *The Birds Our Teachers: essays in orni-theology*, or the theology of birds. He claimed that it is founded on an important biblical principle, that God gave us dominion over the earth and its creatures (Gen. 1:26–28) and Jesus told us to "Look at the birds of the air" (Matt. 6:26). Martin Luther commented "You, see. He is making the birds our school-masters and teachers. ... In other words, we have as many teachers and preachers as there are little birds in the air."[242] Stott also cited Soren Kierkegaard: "So in accordance with the directions of the Gospel let us consider seriously the lilies and the birds as teachers ... and imitate them."[243]

Stott used a variety of birds to teach us about the gospel. In the Sermon on the Mount, Jesus teaches that we should not worry, for the Father feeds the birds so should he not feed us? Stott goes on to correct three common misunderstandings of Jesus' teaching on faith.

First, Jesus is not prohibiting forethought. Some birds store up provisions for the future. Jesus forbids worry, not prudence. Faith in God is not inconsistent with savings and life insurance policies.

Secondly, we are not protected against all accidents, but sparrows do not fall to the ground without our Father's knowledge. Nothing can harm us without our heavenly Father's knowledge and permission.

Thirdly, we are not meant to do nothing to provide for ourselves. Birds feed themselves. God feeds them indirectly. He provides the food but they must forage for it. Faith in God is not incompatible with cooperation with God. Faith and works go together. Salvation is by faith alone but in everything else we both trust God and take appropriate action.[244]

Stott likens repentance to the migration of birds. They "observe the time of their migration" (Jer. 8:7). They fly south in the winter and return in the spring. We also, should return from our self-centered ways to the Lord. Birds have a strong homing instinct and can travel an average 250 miles a day to return to their nest. God is the true home of the human spirit and we are waifs and strays until we return to him.

The owl has the ability to rotate his head 180° and so seeming to face both ways. We too should be able to look back to the past with gratitude and on to the future with expectation. We should not be only futurists and neglect the old and traditional, nor should we be only traditionalists and fail to adapt to change. We should value the first coming of Christ in humility and also look forward to his second coming in glory. When we celebrate the Lord's Supper, we remember his death on the cross and also proclaim his coming again (1 Cor. 11:26).

Self-worth is the lesson of sparrows, in relation to whom Jesus said, "So don't be afraid; you are worth more than many sparrows" (Matt. 10:31; Luke 12:7). Sparrows are a dime a dozen yet Jesus chose this most insignificant bird to compare with us. If we are worth more than the sparrows then we are of value to God. If God cares for the sparrows, how much more does he care for us? Stott repeated his favorite quote of William Temple who said, "my worth is what I am worth to God, and that is a marvelous great deal, for Christ died for me."[245]

Birds can teach us gratitude. Many lift their heads and allow the water to trickle down their throats by gravity. They look as if they are thanking God for the water. We need to lift up our heads in thanksgiving for all God's gifts.

The true gospel of Jesus Christ is that God is able to lift us up and give us the freedom to fly to him. Flight in Scripture is the symbol of salvation. God carried the Israelites from bondage "on eagles' wings" and brought them to himself (Exod. 19:4). We can renew our strength and "soar on wings like eagles" if we wait patiently for the Lord and put our trust in him (Isa. 40:29–31).

A metaphor of God's loving care and protection is the shadow of his wings (Pss. 63:7; 61:4; 57:1; 17:8; 36:7). "He will cover you with his feathers, and under his wings you will find refuge" (Ps. 91:1,4). Jesus wept over Jerusalem that rejected him. "How often I have longed to gather your children together, as a hen gathers her chicks under her wings, and you were not willing!" (Matt. 23:37; Luke 13:34).

Stott concluded his paean to bird life and his lifelong hobby with an appeal to protect and preserve our unique God-given environment. While he grew up and ministered in the great city of London, he escaped, when he could, to his retreat in Pembrokeshire, Wales, called *The Hookses*. He discovered it in 1952 when he went on a camping holiday with John Collins. Eventually he was able to buy it with the proceeds from one of his first books. Over the years he improved it and added on, and it became his retreat where he took friends and did most of his writing. It looks out on West Dale Bay and the Atlantic Ocean. Bird-famous Skokholm Island and Grassholm Island, where 30,000 pairs of gannets nest, lay offshore. He wrote about his passion for birdwatching:

> Birding takes your mind off everything. It rescues you from the noise, the bustle and the pressures of city life, and transplants you into the tranquility of the wilderness. Few experiences are more healing to the spirit than rising with the sun and wandering out into the jungle, the African bush or even an Asian paddyfield, if possible with a friend, but otherwise alone with the sights, the sounds and the smells of nature, and with the living God who conceived and contrived it all.[246]

Stott's ability to enjoy nature and to be renewed by it enabled him to relax and balance his life between work and leisure. He set me an example as a young man by taking me on picnics, to visit his old mentor "Bash" Nash who led him to Christ when he was 17 years old at Rugby School, and by letting me take groups of friends and students to *The Hookses* for retreats. While he churned out books by the dozens and spoke at numerous churches and conferences he was able to find diversion from work and time for relationships in his birding trips and time at *The Hookses*. The theologian was able to do carpentry, stonework, and bricklaying as he developed his coastal property and enlarged it to share with others. His hospitality was legendary.

Epilogue

In March 2008, Antoinette and I joined John Stott at *The Hookses* for a house-party. We knew that this might be the last time to see him. He was nearly 87, frail, in a wheelchair, and needing the help of an attendant friend. Roger Steer was writing a biography of John and wanted our reminiscences. It was published in 2009 as *Inside Story: The Life of John Stott*. When we were leaving we visited John in his study. He was sitting at his desk, before a picture window with a spectacular view of the ocean, working on what would be his last book, *The Radical Disciple: some neglected aspects of our calling*. I remembered how we shared a preaching series at All Souls in the turbulent sixties on "True Radicalism."

This last book reiterates some of the themes Stott championed throughout his ministry: the call to radical nonconformity, to developing a Christian counter-culture, to engagement without compromise. He wrote about the challenges of pluralism, materialism, ethical relativism, and narcissism. He was troubled about church growth without depth and the exploitation of the environment. In response he included the text of "An Evangelical Commitment to a Simple Lifestyle."[247]

The Radical Disciple has a chapter on Christlikeness, based on the text of Stott's final public address, which he gave on 17 July 2007 at the Keswick Convention in the English Lake District. We are to be like Christ in his incarnation, his service, his love, his patient endurance and in his mission. Stott concluded with three practical consequences: the mystery of suffering, the challenge of evangelism, and the indwelling of the Spirit.

In *The Radical Disciple* Stott also shared his experience of falling in 2006 and fracturing his hip, which had to be replaced. His total dependency at that time released in him an emotional weakness that found its expression in weeping. This humiliation led to an acceptance of being dependent on others as he aged, as an analogy of our dependence on the Lord.

The last characteristic of the radical disciple Stott chose to explore is death. Salvation begins with the death of Christ, who calls us to take up our cross and follow him: we are to mortify ourselves by putting to death, or repudiating, our fallen, self-indulgent nature. It is through suffering that the gospel bears fruit. As Stott reflected on death, and in seeking to prepare for it, he turned to Paul's philosophy of life and death: "For to me, to live is Christ and to die is gain" (Phil. 1:21). The life to come will be "far better" than life on earth. "We will be willing to die only when we see the glories of the life to which death leads. This is the radical Christian perspective."[248]

At John Stott's Memorial Service in the College Church in Wheaton, Illinois on 11 November 2011, I closed my remarks remembering his inscription in the Greek-English Lexicon that he gave me to mark my ordination: "Do your best to present yourself to God as one approved, a worker who does not need to be ashamed and who correctly handles the word of truth" (2 Tim. 2:15). This was also John Stott's desire for himself, as expressed in a prayer he habitually said before preaching at All Souls Church:

> *Lord, may your written word be our Rule,*
> *Your Holy Spirit our Teacher, and*
> *Your Glory our supreme concern. Amen.*

Chronological Bibliography

John Stott's books have been published in many editions, and some have been translated into many languages. This list indicates the year of first publication for each of his English titles as well as alternative titles used for the same book.

Bibliographical information refers as far as possible to currently available, in-print editions. Many out-of-print (OP) editions can be accessed in Logos Bible Software.

Further information on books by John Stott and books about him, as well as information on translations, can be found, with links to purchase, at: **www.johnstott100.org** (during 2021, the centenary year of his birth) or at **www.johnstott.org** (ongoing).

John Stott's books (digital) and sermons (audio) are also available in Logos Software at **www.logos.com**

Online audio downloads of his sermons preached at All Souls, Langham Place, London are available from the All Souls Sermon Library at **www.allsouls.org**

Works By or Contributed To by John Stott,
in Order of Their Publication

1950

Becoming a Christian IVP Booklets (Downers Grove, IL: IVP / London: IVP)

1954

Men With a Message: an introduction to the New Testament and its writers / Basic Introduction to the New Testament (Grand Rapids, MI: Eerdmans)

1958

Basic Christianity (London: IVP / Grand Rapids, MI: Eerdmans)

What Christ Thinks of the Church: expository addresses on the first three chapters of the book of Revelation. Re-issued as *What Christ Thinks of the Church: Preaching from Revelation 1 to 3* (2019).

Your Confirmation (London: Hodder & Stoughton). Revised as *Christian Basics: a handbook of beginnings, beliefs and behaviour* (1991).

1961

The Preacher's Portrait: some New Testament word studies. Revised edition published as *The Preacher's Portrait: five NT word studies* (2016).

1964

Being a Christian. IVP Booklets (London: IVP / Downers Grove, IL: IVP)

Confess Your Sins: the way of reconciliation (Grand Rapids, MI: Eerdmans)

The Baptism and Fullness of the Holy Spirit / Baptism and Fullness: the work of the Holy Spirit today (London: IVP / Downers Grove, IL: IVP)

The Epistles of John: an introduction and commentary / The Letters of John: an introduction and commentary. Tyndale NT Commentaries (London: IVP / Downers Grove, IL: IVP)

1966

Men Made New: an exposition of Romans 5–8 (Grand Rapids, MI: Baker). Now included in the BST Commentary on Romans (1994).

The Canticles and Selected Psalms (Prayer Book Commentaries) / *Favourite Psalms* (London: Hodder & Stoughton) OP

1967

Guidelines (London: Falcon). OP

Our Guilty Silence (London: Hodder & Stoughton)

1968

One People: clergy and laity in God's Church (London: Falcon) OP

The Message of Galatians: only one way [*Galatians*]. Bible Speaks Today (BST) Commentaries (London: IVP / Downers Grove, IL: IVP)

1970

Christ the Controversialist: a study in some essentials of evangelical religion / Christ in Conflict (London: IVP / Downers Grove, IL: IVP)

1971

Christ the Liberator by John R.W. Stott and others. Urbana 70 Papers (Downers Grove, IL: IVP) OP

1972

Your Mind Matters: the place of the mind in the Christian life (London: IVP / Downers Grove, IL: IVP)

1973

The Message of 2 Timothy: guard the gospel. Bible Speaks Today (BST) Commentaries (London: IVP / Downers Grove, IL: IVP)

1975

Balanced Christianity (London: IVP / Downers Grove, IL: IVP)

Christian Mission in the Modern World (London: IVP / Downers Grove, IL: IVP). Updated and expanded by Christopher Wright (2015).

The Lausanne Covenant: an exposition and commentary. Re-issued as *The Lausanne Covenant: complete text with study guide*. The Didasko Files (Peabody, MA: Hendrickson / Oxford, UK: Dictum)

1977

Declare His Glory Among the Nations, ed. David Howard (Downers Grove, IL: IVP)

Obeying Christ in a Changing World 1. *The Lord Christ*, ed. John Stott. OP

1978

The Message of the Sermon on the Mount: Christian counter-culture. Bible Speaks Today (BST) Commentaries (London: IVP / Downers Grove, IL: IVP)

1979

Culture and the Bible. OP

Down to Earth: studies in Christianity and culture. Consultation Papers from the Willowbank Consultation on Gospel and Culture. OP

Focus on Christ: an enquiry into the theology of prepositions. Revised as *Life in Christ: a guide for daily living* (2019).

The Message of Ephesians: God's new society. Bible Speaks Today (BST) Commentaries (London: IVP / Downers Grove, IL: IVP)

1982

Between Two Worlds (Grand Rapids, MI: Eerdmans) / *I Believe in Preaching* (London: Hodder & Stoughton). Abbreviated and revised with Greg Scharf as *The Challenge of Preaching* (2011).

God's Book for God's People: why we need the Bible / The Bible: book for today. Revised and updated as *God's Word for Today's World* (2015).

1983

"Jesus Christ, the Life of the World," *Churchman*, Vol. 97, Number 1

1984

Issues Facing Christians Today: new perspectives on social and moral dilemmas / New Issues Facing Christians Today (Grand Rapids, MI: Zondervan)

1985

The Authentic Jesus: a response to current scepticism in the church (London: Marshalls)

1986

The Cross of Christ (London: IVP / Downers Grove, IL: IVP)

The Evangelical-Roman Catholic Dialogue on Mission, eds. Basil Meeking & John Stott. OP

Introduction to Evangelical Preaching: An Anthology of Sermons by Charles Simeon, ed. James Houston (Vancouver: Regent College)

1987

Sermon on the Mount. LifeGuide (Downers Grove, IL: IVP)

1988

Essentials: a liberal-evangelical dialogue, David L. Edwards & John R.W. Stott (London: Hodder & Stoughton) OP

1990

The Message of Acts: the Spirit, the church and the world. Bible Speaks Today (BST) Commentaries (London: IVP / Downers Grove, IL: IVP)

1991

The Message of Thessalonians: the gospel and the end of time. Bible Speaks Today (BST) Commentaries (London: IVP / Downers Grove, IL: IVP)

Christian Basics: a handbook of beginnings, beliefs and behaviour (London: Hodder & Stoughton). Expanded edition of original published as *Your Confirmation* (1958).

1992

The Contemporary Christian: an urgent plea for double listening (London: IVP / Downers Grove, IL: IVP)

1993

The Anglican Communion and Scripture. Papers from the First International Consultation of the Evangelical Fellowship in the Anglican Communion, Canterbury, UK in June 1993. John Stott and others (Regnum, Oxford)

1994

Romans: God's good news for the world. Bible Speaks Today (BST) Commentaries (London: IVP / Downers Grove, IL: IVP). Includes *Men Made New: an exposition of Romans 5–8* (1966).

1995

Authentic Christianity: from the writings of John Stott, ed. Timothy Dudley-Smith (London: IVP / Downers Grove, IL: IVP)

1996

The Message of 1 Timothy and Titus: guard the truth. Bible Speaks Today (BST) Commentaries (London: IVP / Downers Grove, IL: IVP)

Making Christ Known: historic documents from the Lausanne Movement, 1974–89, ed. John Stott. OP

1998

Galatians. John Stott Bible Studies (JSBS) (Downers Grove, IL: IVP)

The Beatitudes. JSBS (Downers Grove, IL: IVP)

1 Timothy & Titus. JSBS (Downers Grove, IL: IVP)

Romans. JSBS (Downers Grove, IL: IVP)

Acts. JSBS (Downers Grove, IL: IVP)

1 & 2 Thessalonians. JSBS (Downers Grove, IL: IVP)

Ephesians. JSBS (Downers Grove, IL: IVP)

Timothy. JSBS (Downers Grove, IL: IVP)

1999

The Birds Our Teachers: essays in orni-theology (Peabody, MA: Hendrickson)

Evangelical Truth: a personal plea for unity and faithfulness (London: IVP / Downers Grove, IL: IVP / Carlisle, UK: Langham Publishing)

2001

The Incomparable Christ (London: IVP / Downers Grove, IL: IVP)

2002

Basic Christian Leadership: biblical models of church, gospel, and ministry (London: IVP / Downers Grove, IL: IVP)

People My Teachers: around the world in eighty years (Grand Rapids, MI: Kregel)

2004

The Grace of Giving: 10 principles of Christian giving. The Didasko Files (Peabody, MA: Hendrickson / Oxford, UK: Dictum). Expanded by Christopher Wright and James Cousins as *Shortfall: owning the challenge of ministry funding* (2021).

2006

Through the Bible Through the Year (Oxford, UK: Lion Hudson)

2007

Living Church : convictions of a lifelong pastor (London: IVP / Downers Grove, IL: IVP)

2008

Revelation. JSBS (Downers Grove, IL: IVP)
Jesus Christ. JSBS (Downers Grove, IL: IVP)
The Anglican Evangelical Doctrine of Infant Baptism, John Stott & Alec Motyer (London: Latimer Trust)

2009

The Cross. LifeGuide (Downers Grove, IL: IVP)

2010

The Radical Disciple: wholehearted Christian living (London: IVP) / *The Radical Disciple: some neglected aspects of our calling* (Downers Grove, IL: IVP)

2011

The Challenge of Preaching, with Greg Scharf (Carlisle, UK: Langham Publishing / Grand Rapids, MI: Eerdmans). First published as *I Believe in Preaching / Between Two Worlds* (1982).

2012

Evangelical Truth: A personal plea for unity, integrity and faithfulness, with The Cape Town Commitment of the Third Lausanne Congress (London, UK: IVP / Carlisle, UK: Langham Publishing)

2014

Challenges of Christian Leadership: practical wisdom for leaders, interwoven with the author's advice (London: IVP / Downers Grove, IL: IVP)

2015

God's Word for Today's World (Carlisle, UK: Langham Publishing). First published as *The Bible: book for today* (1982).
Christian Mission in the Modern World, by Christopher Wright (London: IVP / Downers Grove, IL: IVP). Expanded edition of the original published by John Stott (1975).

2016

The Preacher's Portrait: five NT word studies (Carlisle, UK: Langham Publishing / Grand Rapids, MI: Eerdmans). First published in 1961 as *The Preacher's Portrait: some New Testament word studies.*

2019

Christ the Cornerstone: collected essays of John Stott (Bellingham, WA: Lexham Press)

Life in Christ: a guide for daily living (Carlisle, UK: Langham Publishing). First published as *Focus on Christ* in 1979.

What Christ Thinks of the Church: preaching from Revelation 1 to 3 (Carlisle, UK: Langham Publishing). First published in 1958.

2020

Pages from a Preacher's Notebook: wisdom and prayers from the pen of John Stott, ed. Mark Meynell (Bellingham, WA: Lexham Press)

2021

Shortfall: owning the challenge of ministry funding (Carlisle, UK: Langham Publishing). Expanded edition of *The Grace of Giving: 10 principles of Christian giving* by John Stott (2004).

Books About John Stott

Christopher Catherwood, *Five Evangelical Leaders* (1985) (Fearn, UK: Christian Focus, 1994)

Martyn Eden, ed. & David Wells, *The Gospel in the Modern World: a tribute to John Stott* (Downers Grove, IL: IVP / London: IVP, 1991)

Timothy Dudley-Smith, *John Stott, The Making of a Leader: a biography, the early years* (Downers Grove, IL: IVP / London: IVP, 1999)

Timothy Dudley-Smith, *John Stott, A Global Ministry: a biography, the later years* (Downers Grove, IL: IVP / London: IVP, 2001)

Roger Steer, *Inside Story: the life of John Stott* (London: IVP, 2009) / *Basic Christian: the inside story of John Stott* (Downers Grove, IL: IVP, 2009)

Christopher J.H. Wright, ed., *Portraits of a Radical Disciple: recollections of John Stott's life and ministry* (London: IVP, 2011) / *John Stott: A Portrait by his Friends* (Downers Grove, IL: IVP, 2011)

Alister Chapman, *Godly Ambition: John Stott and the Evangelical Movement* (Oxford, UK: OUP, 2012)

Chris Wright, *John Stott: pastor, teacher, friend* (Peabody, MA: Hendrickson, 2012)

Julia Cameron, *John Stott: the humble leader* (Fearn, UK: Christian Focus, 2012)

David Cranston, *John Stott & The Hookses* (Oxford, UK: Words by Design, 2017)

Tim Chester, *Stott on the Christian Life: between two worlds* (Wheaton, IL: Crossway, 2020)

Endnotes

John Stott's publications have had many editions, co-publisher activity and in some cases revisions or expansions. The information in these Notes relates to the (hardcopy) editions the author quotes from; information for the most current in-print editions appear in the Chronological Bibliography.

Chapter 3: The Holy Spirit

Introduction

1. Timothy Dudley-Smith, ed. and John R.W. Stott, *Authentic Christianity* (Downers Grove: IVP, 1996) p.10
2. William Carus, *Memoirs of the Rev. Charles Simeon* (New York: Robert Carter, 1847) p.131
3. *Ibid.*, p.488
4. See, for example, his *Your Mind Matters* (IVP, 1972)
5. John Stott, *Through the Bible Through the Year* (Oxford: Monarch, 2014, 2nd edn; first published in 2006) p.353

Chapter 1: God

6. John Stott, *Christian Basics: a handbook of beginnings, beliefs and behavior* (Grand Rapids: Baker, 1991) summary of pp.57–61
7. *Through the Bible* (2014) p.296
8. *Christian Basics* (1991) pp.54–56
9. John Stott, *The Message of Ephesians: God's new society*, Bible Speaks Today (BST) commentaries (Downers Grove: IVP, 1979) p.52
10. *Through the Bible* (2014) p.2
11. John Stott, *The Cross of Christ* (Downers Grove: IVP, 1986) p.106
12. John Stott, *The Canticles and Selected Psalms* (London: Hodder & Stoughton, 1966) p.46

Chapter 2: Christ

13. John Stott, *Basic Christianity* (Grand Rapids: Eerdmans, 1964 edn of the 1958 first edn) pp.19–21
14. *Ibid.*, pp.32,33
15. *Ibid.*, pp.42,43
16. John Stott, *The Authentic Jesus: a response to current scepticism in the church* (London: Marshalls, Morgan and Scott, 1985) pp.29,30
17. *The Authentic Jesus* (1985) p.34
18. *Ibid.*, pp.73–78
19. John Stott, *Focus on Christ: an enquiry into the theology of prepositions* (London: Fount Paperbacks, 1979) pp.11,15

20 This article was subsequently included in *Christ the Cornerstone: collected essays of John Stott* (Ashland: Lexham Press, 2019) p.303
21 *Basic Christianity* (1964) p.102
22 *Ibid.*, p.79
23 *Christian Basics* (1991) pp.78–86
24 John Stott, *The Baptism and Fullness of the Holy Spirit* (Chicago: IVP, 1964) p.3
25 *Ibid.*, p.4
26 *Ibid.*, p.10
27 *Ibid.*, p.13
28 *Ibid.*, pp.23,24
29 *Ibid.*, pp.34,35
30 John R.W. Stott and others, *Christ the Liberator*, Urbana 70 Papers (Downers Grove: IVP, 1971) p.43
31 *Ibid.*, p.44. The reference to R.V.G. Tasker is from his *The Gospel According to John* (Grand Rapids: Eerdmans, 1960) pp.179,180
32 *Christ the Liberator* (1971) pp.45,46

Chapter 4: Humanity

33 John R.W. Stott, *Christ the Controversialist: a study in some essentials of evangelical religion* (London: Tyndale Press, 1970) pp.45,46. [Published by IVP, US: *Christ in Conflict*, 1970.
34 *Ibid.*, pp.139–142
35 John R.W. Stott, *Men Made New: an exposition of Romans 5–8* (Grand Rapids: Baker, 1984; first published in 1966) p.24
36 David L. Edwards and John R.W. Stott, *Essentials: a liberal-evangelical dialogue* (London: Hodder & Stoughton, 1988) p.262
37 *Men Made New* (1984, first published 1966) p.24
38 John R.W. Stott, *Romans: God's good news for the world*, Bible Speaks Today (BST) commentaries (Downers Grove: IVP, 1994) pp.162–66
39 *Basic Christianity* (1964) pp.63,64
40 *Ibid.*, pp.72–81
41 Article IX of the Articles of Religion, *Book of Common Prayer*
42 *Basic Christianity* (1964) pp.76,77
43 William Temple, *Christianity and Social Order* (London: Penguin, 1942) pp.36,37
44 *Romans* (BST, 1994) pp.100–105.
45 John R.W. Stott, *The Message of the Sermon on the Mount: Christian counter-culture*, Bible Speaks Today (BST) commentaries (Leicester, UK: IVP, 1978) p.120
46 *Romans* (BST, 1994) p.104
47 James M. Houston, ed., *Evangelical Preaching: an anthology of sermons by Charles Simeon* (Vancouver: Regent College Publishing, 2003) p.xxxix
48 *The Message of Ephesians* (BST, 1979) p.72
49 Ibid., p.80

Chapter 5: The Cross

50 *The Cross of Christ* (1986) p.83
51 *Ibid.*, p.112
52 Emil Brunner, *The Mediator: a study of the central doctrine of the Christian faith* (Macmillan, 1934) pp.444,445. Stott goes on to cite Brunner 10 times.
53 *Ibid.*, p.485
54 *Ibid.*, p.519
55 *Ibid.*, pp.281,282
56 *Ibid.*, p.467

57 *Ibid.*, p.450
58 *Ibid.*, p.470
59 *Ibid.*, p.520
60 *The Cross of Christ* (1986) p.132
61 *Ibid.*, p.151
62 *Ibid.*, p.156
63 *Ibid.*, p.160
64 *Romans* (BST, 1994) pp.113–18. Here Stott quotes from Brunner, *The Mediator*, pp.291–94
65 *Ibid.*, p.338
66 *Ibid.*, p.322
67 *Ibid.*, p.328
68 *Ibid.*, p.335

Chapter 6: The Holy Scriptures

69 Carus, *Memoirs* (1847) p.15
70 J.I. Packer, ed., *Guidelines: Anglican evangelicals face the future*, Conference papers in preparation for the National Evangelical Anglican Congress of April 1967 (London: Falcon Books, 1967) p.42
71 Packer, ed., *Guidelines* (1967) pp.51,52. The references are to Riesenfeld's *The Gospel Tradition and its Beginnings* (London: Mowbray, 1961) and Gerhardsson's *Memory and Manuscript* (Lund: Gleerup, 1964)
72 Packer, ed., *Guidelines* (1967) p.63
73 John Stott, *The Message of Galatians: only one way*, Bible Speaks Today (BST) commentaries (Downers Grove: IVP, 1968) pp.15,16; the Dodd quote is from his *The Epistle to the Romans*, Moffat New Testament Commentary (Hodder, 1932) pp.xxxiv,xxxv
74 *The Message of Galatians* (BST, 1968) p.16
75 Edwards and Stott, *Essentials* (1988) p.268
76 John Stott, *The Contemporary Christian: an urgent plea for double listening* (Downers Grove: IVP, 1992) p.186
77 *Ibid.*, p.196
78 *Ibid.*, pp.205,206
79 John Stott, *The Lausanne Covenant: complete text with study guide* (Peabody, Mass: Hendrickson, 2009) p.16

Chapter 7: Salvation

80 John R.W. Stott, *Christian Mission in the Modern World: what the church should be doing now!* (Downers Grove: IVP, 1975) p.8
81 *Ibid.*
82 *Ibid.*
83 *Ibid.*, pp.86,87. The Lloyd-Jones quote is from a Christian Medical Fellowship booklet "Will hospital replace the Church?", 1969
84 *Christian Mission in the Modern World* (1975), p.89
85 *Ibid.*, p.95
86 *The Contemporary Christian* (1992) p.310
87 Timothy Dudley-Smith, *John Stott, A Global Ministry: a biography, the later years* (Downers Grove 2001) p.206
88 *Basic Christianity* (1964) p.100
89 John R.W. Stott, *The Message of 2 Timothy: guard the gospel*, Bible Speaks Today (BST) commentaries (Downers Grove: IVP, 1973) p.35
90 *Romans* (BST, 1994) pp.250–52

91 *The Message of 2 Timothy* (BST, 1973) pp.36–40
92 John Stott, "The Messenger of God: Studies in Romans 1–5", in J.W. Alexander, ed., *Believing and Obeying Jesus Christ* (Downers Grove: IVP, 1980) p.103
93 John R.W. Stott, *The Epistles of John: an introduction and commentary*, Tyndale New Testament Commentaries (London: Tyndale Press, 1964) p.50
94 *Christian Basics* (1991) pp.29–36
95 John Stott, *The Message of 1 Timothy and Titus: guard the truth*, Bible Speaks Today (BST) commentaries (Downers Grove: IVP, 1996) p.201
96 *Ibid.*, pp.207,208

Chapter 8: The Church

97 Timothy Dudley-Smith, *John Stott, The Making of a Leader: a biography, the early years* (Downers Grove: IVP, 1999) p.255
98 John Stott, *Between Two Worlds: the art of preaching in the twentieth century* (Grand Rapids: Eerdmans, 1982; published by Hodder & Stoughton as *I Believe in Preaching*) p.109
99 *Through the Bible Through the Year* (2014) p.306
100 *The Message of Galatians* (BST, 1968) p.180
101 John Stott, *One People* (Downers Grove: IVP, 1968) p.15
102 *Ibid.*, pp.20–23
103 *Ibid.*, pp.20–23
104 *Through the Bible* (2014) p.305
105 *The Message of Ephesians* (BST, 1979) p.9
106 *Ibid.*, p.27
107 *Ibid.*, p.126
108 *Ibid.*, pp.127,128
109 *The Epistles of John* (Tyndale NT Commentaries, 1964) p.63
110 *One People* (1968) pp.83–91
111 *Christian Basics* (1991) p.47
112 John Stott, *What Christ Thinks of the Church: insight from Revelation 2–3* (Grand Rapids: Eerdmans, 1972; first publ in 1958) pp.40–45
113 *Ibid.*, p.79
114 *Ibid.*, p.88
115 *Ibid.*, pp.116,117
116 *Christ the Liberator* (1971) pp.87,88. Another analysis of John 17 may be found in Chapter 16 of *The Contemporary Christian* (1992) pp.261–69. An interesting example of Stott's concern for this subject is his participation in the Evangelical-Roman Catholic Dialogue on Mission 1977–84. A Report of its meetings was published in 1986.
117 John Stott, *The Living Church: convictions of a lifelong pastor* (Downers Grove: IVP, 2007) p.164
118 *Christianity Today* (8 January 1996) p.27
119 *The Living Church* (2007) pp.167–69

Chapter 9: Preaching

120 John Stott, *The Preacher's Portrait: some New Testament word studies* (London: Tyndale Press, 1961) p.21
121 *Ibid.*, pp.24,25
122 *Ibid.*, p.36
123 *Ibid.*, p.37
124 *Ibid.*, pp.43,44
125 *Ibid.*, pp.48,49

[126] E.H. Plumptre, 1821–1891
[127] *The Preacher's Portrait* (1961) p.54
[128] *Ibid.*, p.57
[129] *Ibid.*, p.66
[130] *Ibid.*, pp.68; E.M. Bounds quote from *Power Through Prayer*, p.11
[131] *The Preacher's Portrait* (1961) p.70
[132] *Ibid.*, pp.78,79
[133] *Ibid.*, p.81
[134] J.C. Ryle, *The Christian Leaders of England in the Last Century* (Chas J. Thynne Popular Edition, 1902) pp.24,25 as quoted by Stott
[135] *The Preacher's Portrait* (1961), p.83
[136] *Ibid.*, p.85
[137] R. Baxter, *The Reformed Pastor* (Epworth Press, 2nd ed, revised 1950) p.162
[138] *The Preacher's Portrait* (1961) pp.90,91
[139] *Ibid.*, pp.97–105
[140] *Ibid.*, p.106
[141] *Ibid.*, pp.109–11
[142] *Between Two Worlds* (1982) p.92
[143] *Ibid.*, p.93
[144] *Ibid.*, p.97
[145] *Ibid.*, p.99
[146] *Ibid.*, p.109
[147] *Ibid.*, p.115
[148] *Ibid.*, p121, from Ramsey, *The Christian Priest*, p.7
[149] *Between Two Worlds* (1982), p.126
[150] *Between Two Worlds* (1982) p.130
[151] C. Simeon, *Horae Homileticae*, p.12
[152] It was abridged by Greg Scharf and reprinted in 2011 by Langham, UK.
[153] *The Contemporary Christian* (1992) p.13
[154] *Between Two Worlds* (1982) p.151
[155] *Ibid.*, p.154
[156] *Ibid.*, p.167
[157] *Ibid.*, pp.170,171
[158] *Ibid.*, pp.177,178

Chapter 10: The Sacraments

[159] *Christ the Controversialist* (1970) p.102
[160] John Stott & Alec Motyer, *The Anglican Evangelical Doctrine of Infant Baptism* (London: Latimer Trust, 2008). This is a joint publication of "The Evangelical Doctrine of Baptism" by John Stott and "Baptism in the Book of Common Prayer" by Alec Motyer.
[161] *Ibid.*, p.8
[162] *Ibid.*, p.9
[163] *Ibid.*, p.11, attributed to St. Augustine
[164] *Ibid.*, pp.20,21
[165] *Christian Basics* (1991) p.132
[166] Latimer *Works*, ii.286
[167] An Evangelical Open Letter on ARCIC, addressed to the Anglican Episcopate, Easter 1988

Chapter 11: Mission

[168] John Stott, *Our Guilty Silence: the church, the gospel and the world* (London: Hodder & Stoughton, 1967) p.13

[169] *Ibid.*, p.15

[170] *Ibid.*, pp.25–26

[171] *Ibid.*, p.32

[172] *Ibid.*, p.37

[173] *Ibid.*, p.117

[174] First published in 1975. This book was updated and expanded by Stott and Christopher J.H. Wright in 2015 to show how Stott's thoughts on mission had continued to develop.

[175] *Christian Mission in the Modern World* (1975) p.23

[176] David M. Howard, ed., *Declare His Glory Among the Nations*, Conference Papers (Downers Grove: IVP, 1977) pp.31–91

[177] *Ibid.*, p.34

[178] *Ibid.*, p.53

[179] *Ibid.*, p.78

[180] *The Contemporary Christian* (1992) p.339

[181] *Ibid.*, p.351, from King, *Strength To Love* (Collins, 1963) p.34

[182] *Christianity Today* 23, no. 7 (5 January 1979) pp.34–35; the article was republished in *Christ the Cornerstone* (2019) pp.108–13

[183] *The Contemporary Christian* (1992) p.373

[184] John Stott, *Culture and the Bible* (Downers Grove: IVP, 1979) p.40

[185] John Stott, ed., *Making Christ Known: historic documents from the Lausanne Movement, 1974–1989* (Grand Rapids: Eerdmans, 1996) p.87

[186] *Culture and the Bible* (1979) p.45

[187] John Stott and Robert Coote, eds, *Down to Earth: studies in Christianity and culture* (Grand Rapids: Eerdmans, 1979) p.viii

Chapter 12: Discipleship

[188] See *Christian Basics* (1991) pp.21–23

[189] A radical summary from *Basic Christianity* (1964) pp.111–20

[190] *Ibid.*, pp.123,124

[191] *Ibid.*, pp.124–29

[192] *Ibid.*, p.131

[193] *Christian Basics* (1991) pp.38–39

[194] *Ibid.*, pp.40–44

[195] *Ibid.*, p.40

[196] *Ibid.*, p.41

[197] *Ibid.*, p.43

[198] *Ibid.*, p.44

[199] *Ibid.*, pp.118–23

[200] *The Message of Galatians* (BST, 1968) p.150

[201] *Ibid.*

[202] *Ibid.*, pp.150–52

[203] *Ibid.*, pp.169,170

[204] *Ibid.*, p.190

[205] *Christ the Liberator* (1971) pp.25,26

[206] *Ibid.*, p.53; the Muggeridge quote is from his *Jesus Rediscovered* (Glasgow: Collins-Fontana, 1969) pp.158,159

[207] J.C. Ryle, *Expository Thoughts*, p.335

[208] D. Bonhoeffer, *Cost of Discipleship* (London: Macmillan, 1937) p.74

[209] *Christ the Liberator* (1971) p.65, quoting from Muggeridge, *Jesus Rediscovered*, p.91
[210] *The Message of Ephesians* (BST, 1979) pp.193,194
[211] *The Message of the Sermon on the Mount* (BST, 1978) p.54
[212] *Ibid.*, pp.210,211
[213] *The Lausanne Covenant: an exposition and commentary* (World Wide Publications, 1975) p.41
[214] *The Lausanne Covenant: study guide* (2009) pp.41,42
[215] John Stott, *The Radical Disciple: some neglected aspects of our calling* (Downers Grove: IVP, 2010)

Chapter 13: The Kingdom of God
[216] John Stott, *Basic Introduction to the New Testament* (Grand Rapids: Eerdmans, 1964, 1985; first published in 1954 as *Men with a Message*) pp.4–22
[217] *The Message of Ephesians* (BST, 1979) p.105
[218] *Making Christ Known* (1996) p.187
[219] *Ibid.*, pp.187–90

Chapter 14: Ethics
[220] John Stott, *Issues Facing Christians Today: a major appraisal of contemporary social and moral questions* (Basingstoke: Marshalls, 1984) pp.xi,xii
[221] Temple, *Christianity and Social Order* (Penguin, 1942) p.41
[222] *Ibid.*, p.29
[223] *The Christian Mind* (London: SPCK, 1963) p.43
[224] Republished in *Christ the Cornerstone* (2019) p.248
[225] *Ibid.*, p.295
[226] *Romans* (BST, 1994) pp.77,78
[227] Charles Cranfield, *Romans 1* (Edinburgh: T. and T. Clark, 1975) p.125
[228] Dudley-Smith, *John Stott, A Global Ministry* (2001) p.395

Chapter 15: The Last Things
[229] Edwards and Stott, *Essentials* (1988) p.306
[230] *Christ the Liberator* (1971) pp.34–37
[231] *Ibid.*, p.37
[232] Edwards and Stott, *Essentials* (1988) pp.307,308
[233] *Basic Introduction to the New Testament* (1964) pp.173,174
[234] Edwards and Stott, *Essentials* (1988) pp.308–309
[235] *Ibid.*, pp.315–20
[236] *Christianity Today* (8 January 1996) p.28; an interview Roy McCloughry entitled "Basic Stott: candid comments on justice, gender, and judgement"
[237] *The Cross of Christ* (1986) pp.89–110
[238] Paragraph 14.
[239] Edwards and Stott, *Essentials* (1988) pp.321–27; quoting Norman Anderson, *Christianity and World Religions: the challenge of pluralism* (Downers Grove: IVP, 1984) p.153
[240] Edwards and Stott, *Essentials* (1988) pp.327–28

Chapter 16: Orni-Theology
[241] John Stott, *The Birds Our Teachers: essays in orni-theology* (Wheaton: Harold Shaw, 1999) p.8

[242] Martin Luther (1521), "The Sermon on the Mount," trans. by Jaroslav Pelikan, *Luther's Works* 21 (Concordia, 1956) pp.197,198

[243] S. Kierkegaard, trans. Walter Lowrie, *Christian Discourses and the Lilies of the Field and the Birds of the Air* (London: Oxford University Press, 1940) p.311

[244] *The Birds Our Teachers* (1999) pp.12–14

[245] *Ibid.*, pp. 24,25,38

[246] David Cranston, *John Stott and the Hookses* (Words by Design, 2017) p.15

Epilogue

[247] "An Evangelical Commitment to Simple LifeStyle" was written and endorsed by the International Consultation on Simple LifeStyle, held at Hoddesdon, England, 17–21 March 1980. The consultation was sponsored by the World Evangelical Fellowship Theological Commission's Unit on Ethics and Society (Dr. Ronald Sider, Chairman) and the Lausanne Committee on World Evangelization's Lausanne Theology and Education Group (Rev. John Stott, Chairman). The document in its entirety was included in *The Radical Disciple* (2010) pp.64–82.

[248] *The Radical Disciple* (2010) pp.130–33

Also by Ted Schroder

Inward Light

Buried Treasure

Surviving Hurricanes

Solid Love

Real Hope

Why Am I?

Encouragement in a World of Hurt

Soul Food: Daily Devotions for the Hungry, Vols. 1, 2, 3, 4

Peace of Mind

Why I Believe in Jesus Christ

*What Is The Importance And Significance of the
Lord's Supper Or Holy Communion?*

Day by Day with Ted SchroderAdd after this:

And, with R. Waugh, S. Lowe, A. Davidson,
God Knows Where They Come From: four faith stories from Hokitika

www.tedschroder.com

CPSIA information can be obtained
at www.ICGtesting.com
Printed in the USA
LVHW030328250821
696016LV00002B/16

9 781909 281882